Hand Me Down

Hand Me Down

By

Geoffrey Allen

Chi Media Company
Milpitas CA

Cover by Zach McCain

ISBN 13: 978-1-7354908-4-7

Second Edition

CHI MEDIA
COMPANY

For Nita

Part I: Chapter One

Louis was a successful bond trader working on Wall Street. He was forty-three and had been earning more than a seven-figure income since he was thirty. But lately, Louis felt that the trading routine was losing its appeal. He wanted to do something different. He wanted to make a difference in the world. To make his mark, to contribute to society and leave a lasting impression on his children.

There was only one problem, however.

Louis had no fucking idea what to do.

His entire life had been sucked into a monotonous routine—rise at 3:30 am, turn on the TV, get on the Internet, call places like London and Asia, make a full array of trades. All to satisfy his clients' wishes for unhinged monetary growth. This was how Louis lived his life.

When he was thirty-eight, he married Donna, a beautiful administrative assistant who was bright and had a fantastic body, but most importantly, had an outstanding sense of humor. She was a good mother to their two children, Felix and Michelle. There was no question that life was good…but something had been lacking.

One night, when Louis arrived home from work, he announced to Donna that he wanted to make a difference in the world. She was at the kitchen table, breastfeeding Michelle, while the nanny played chess with Felix. The TV and stereo were both on simultaneously, filling the air with a pulse of disharmony.

Donna, loyal wife that she was, smiled at her husband upon hearing his words. "Honey, I support you a hundred percent."

Louis' shoulders relaxed and he smiled back at his wife.

Donna went on. "I've always trusted your judgment immensely...but, honey, look around you. You *have* made a difference.

The features on Louis' face darkened as he realized what his wife was saying to him. "This isn't the differ ence I'm talking about. The $30 million in the bank, the four-bedroom coop in Manhattan, the second home in the Hamptons—it's all just bullshit."

Stunned by Louis' tone, Donna looked up at him, speechless.

Realizing he'd upset his wife, Louis lowered his voice. "I'm just saying—Look...I'm already taking all this medicine for my blood pressure; not to mention, for my cholesterol and triglycerides. I just don't want to drop dead before I'm fifty."

Donna's smile reappeared on her face, as if it had always been there. "You won't, sweetheart. You're just stressed out. It happens to all of us. Just take it one day at a time."

With that, Donna went back to breastfeeding the baby.

Louis sighed to himself and exited the kitchen.

Louis and Donna owned a co-op. It was located on Manhattan's Upper East Side. Their neighborhood supposedly boasted the most affluen zip code in the world. The apartment was a two-level duplex and had about four-thousand square feet of living space. The view from the living room was breathtaking, overlooking all of Central Park. And a corner room had views of both the Hudson and East rivers.

At 8:30 pm, Louis went to his home office on the second level of the coop, to wrap up some west coast transactions before going to bed. After that, he took a sleeping pill, put on his eye mask, and fell asleep before 9:30 pm. Such was the routine every single night.

At one point, Louis woke up to take a piss. He squinted at the clock and saw that it was 11:30 pm. He was thankful that he had four more hours before he had to get up.

Then, at 2:30 am, Louis got up to take another leak.

He thought to himself: *Those goddamn diuretics. They're controlling my blood pressure, but I'm constantly urinating. Maybe I should wear adult pampers. Perhaps that will be my legacy to my children: That I couldn't sleep through the night because I was constantly urinating. I could be the poster child for the largest adult diaper manufacturer in North America. My kids would see me on the billboards, on TV and on YouTube; I could even go to Felix's preschool class and talk to the students about my inability to hold my water at age forty-three.*

Not much later, at 3:30 am, the alarm blared, and Louis sprang out of bed, tripping over one of the kids' toys in the process. He had not taken off his night mask timely enough. He wobbled to the bathroom and turned on the shower, which was not, by any means, an ordinary shower.

First of all, the bathroom surrounding it was about a thousand square feet. The shower alone was ten by twelve. One wall was completely made of glass. There was a drawer inside the wall that contained all the items that Louis needed to wash and shave. The other wall was unusual, as it was a Giant TV screen, positioned behind a solid glass covering.

Louis turned on CNBC and let the day begin.

He was out of the bathroom in twenty minutes. He went into his gigantic closet to get his clothes. No question about it, Louis had fabulous clothes. His suits, ties, and shirts were all handmade in London. But the one thing that Louis really had a passion for was shoes—he had two hundred pairs. Secretly, he had waged a silent competition between Imelda Marcos and himself. Also, his suits were immaculate. Some of them cost around ten grand; not only that, but the tailoring was done by one of the fin est craftsmen alive.

Louis put his outfit of the day on his suit caddy. He

then went back into the bedroom and stared at Donna as she slept in bed.

Maybe I should play hooky from work. I could stay home and fuck the shit out of Donna all day, he thought to himself.

Donna's body was incredible. She was a year younger than Louis, and had long beautiful legs, a nice firm ass, and breasts that were always at attention. Her skin was milk white and her complexion fla less, even without makeup. Before leaving the room, Louis thought about how fortunate a man he was.

He went to his home offic and turned on his computer, along with the four monitors that were strategically located on each wall. In order to keep up with the different markets, he had monitors for the US, Europe, Asia, and basic use of the Internet; all of them were tied to his main office on all Street.

He began making his calls to Asia to do some trades. Louis was fluent in Taiwanese and spoke in the native tongue to the other traders working thousands of miles away. By 4:30 am, he had already done nine trades. He continued this ritual until 5:15 am and then he started putting his suit on. Within twenty minutes, Louis was meticulously dressed and ready to face the day. He looked like the epitome of success. His entire outfit probably cost him around $25,000. Not to mention, his Girard-Perregaux watch was worth about $200,000.

Louis was now ready to conquer the streets and make his day's fortune. He stepped into the kitchen and brewed some hazelnut coffee. He poured himself a cup and started to sip. Louis always ate breakfast at the office He had a personal chef that cooked him breakfast and lunch when he was in the building. When Louis met with clients, he always took them out to a restaurant near the office However, as Louis was watching his weight, he actually preferred to have the chef prepare all of his meals for him.

At 5:55 am, Louis left the coop and got into the elevator, which led him to the lobby. He said "good morning" to the doorman, Alfie, and moved swiftly out the door to his limo.

Inside the limo sat his faithful driver, William. A friend and a confidant, William had been Louis' driver for the past fifteen years. He knew everything under the sun about him. He even served as Louis' personal shrink, during challenging times.

"Good morning, William."

"Good morning, Mr. Bexton."

The drive to Wall Street from uptown was about half an hour.

A copy of the Wall Street Journal and a bottle of water were waiting for Louis inside the limo. William had also made sure that the small TV was tuned in to CNBC.

On most drives, there was little conversation between the two men—unless Louis initiated it. This would be one such drive.

"William, can I ask you something?"

"Of course, Mr. Bexton."

"Well…lately I've been feeling that I'd like to make a difference in the world. But I haven't a clue as to what I should do," Louis muttered, looking down into his lap.

"You want to make a difference, Mr. Bexton? Then why don't you give me $10 million as a gift? We would be on the cover of the *New York Post.* 'Trader Makes a Difference: Gives his Driver $10 Million,'" William said, breaking out into a big smile.

Louis couldn't help but smile back at his friend. "Come on, I'm being serious here."

"Okay…what about charitable organizations? I'm sure there are a lot of charities out there that could use your talents and business savvy. It's worth asking around."

Louis nodded at his friend. "Yeah, maybe. I'll think about it."

With that, Louis went about initiating a couple of trades on his wireless laptop. In time, they pulled up to his office

"Would you come pick me up at six?" Louis asked.

"Of course, Mr. Bexton. I'll be here," William replied.

Louis hopped out of the limo and shut the door behind him. The car sped away through a quiet downtown district.

Louis entered the building, swiped his fob for security purposes, and stepped into the elevator. Within a minute, he was on the thirty-sixth floor. He entered the main entrance using his fob. No one was at the reception desk, as the offic was not officiall open until 8:30 am. Above the desk was a sign with the firm name, Golden, Mellow, and Wasberger; it was barely visible as there were only a few lights on in the office

Louis had never had any interest in being a partner, so it didn't bother him that his name was not on the firm's sign. Louis, after all, was the rainmaker. He made more than $250,000,000 for the firm last year alone. His keep was four percent, which earned him a cool $10,000,000, not to mention a handsome bonus. Louis was fine with making deals and doing trades, but he had no interest in the administrative aspects of the job. He disliked atten-ing meetings and did not want to serve at any supervisory capacity. Management was simply not for him.

Louis' offic was a corner office whereas many of the traders sat in cubicles in the middle of an open area. Louis' God-like status secured for him the comfort of his own office which overlooked the Hudson River. The offic was, surprisingly, relatively barren. His desk was an antique oak "partner's" desk with a polished top. It was a piece that he and Donna picked out when they were on one of their antique journeys in New York State. Four phones sat atop his desk. There was also one computer with three monitors attached to it. On the southern wall of the offic was a large plasma TV.

Upon arriving in his office Louis flipped on the lights, turned on the TV, and sat in an unpretentious leather chair. During his first call to Taiwan, he initiated a currency trade in the Huang for a client. While speaking fluent Taiwanese, Louis adroitly managed the trading details like a fine symphony conductor playing at Carnegie Hall. This particular client wanted to short on the Huang and bet that it would drop against the US dollar. Louis encouraged his client to do it, as his research dictated that this was the way to go in the current economic climate. The client wanted it to be a short-term trade; he instructed Louis to sell within minutes. Louis placed the Huang on his alert list, which connected to his desktop computer, landline, cell phone, and beeper. All rang simultaneously if any movement occurred. Louis needed the variety of sources because he never knew where he would be at any given time. There could be a major drop and Louis could be on the throne, taking a dump, which would likely preclude him from taking advantage of the opportunity.

Louis' next call was to the UK, where he was buying warrants on the London Stock Exchange for a client. He had to position his Asian and European trades before 9 am Eastern Standard Time, so he could get ready for his domestic trading. His primary domestic trading venue was commodities, where the profit potential was the most lucrative. But Louis' area of expertise was trading platinum; this is where he made over eighty percent of his income. After the UK call, Louis swept the internet for any details on the platinum market, because he had to be aware of the trends, as well as the short-term and long-term outlooks. He sometimes also received internal emails from the firm to update him on the market conditions surrounding platinum. Louis read the firm emails, but he mostly relied on his own research and familiarity with the platinum market.

As Louis kept his door closed, he was unable to hear the stirring of the people starting to fill the offic outside. He was generally a loner and was very focused on the task at hand; he had very little time (and need) for social intercourse.

At 9:15 am there was a knock at the door, and in came an administrative assistant named Sally. She was dressed seductively in a low-cut top, short mini-skirt, mesh stockings, and spiked heels. She looked at Louis and asked, "Mr. Bexton, is there anything I can get you this morning?"

"Sure," Louis responded. "Can you order me lunch? Turkey on whole wheat, and...lettuce, tomatoes, and mustard."

"Anything to drink?"

"I'll have a diet ginger ale."

It was hard for Louis to stay focused when Sally entered his office She was a beautiful woman in her late twenties. Rumor had it that Mr. Golden, the firm founder, was nailing her on a pretty regular basis.

When Sally turned and walked out of the office Louis couldn't help but stare at her magnificent legs. But he quickly averted his attention back toward his rainmaking activities. Sally closed the door behind her, but he could still smell a trace of her tantalizing perfume. He thought to himself: *Definite widow-maker material.*

Since Louis was on diuretics for his blood pressure, he frequented the bathroom regularly. The firm gave him his own private john, located in his office At around 11 am Louis was in the bathroom, sitting on the throne, when his beeper and cell phone started ringing at the same time. Louis checked his phone and saw a text message stating that there was a major correction in the Huang as a result of an impending Tsunami in Asia. He had no time to wipe, nor—for that matter—button up his pants properly

Proper hygiene would have to take a backseat for now.

He ran to his desk and went to his computer to enter the sell order on the Huang.

Waited for a few seconds...then...

Done.

One hour later, he received the confirmation that the trade had settled. And it was that simple. Louis had made a $2 million profit for his client. He punched a few numbers on his calculator. The number *80,000* appeared on the screen. That was the dollar amount of what the Bexton

household would be taking in.
The adrenaline was now flowing
Louis was at the peak of his game.

Chapter Two

William picked Louis up from his offic at 6 pm. When Louis got situated in the limo, he called his wife.

"Hi, honey. I just wanted to remind you…tonight's poker night with the guys and I won't be home till after midnight."

Donna let out a casual sigh on the other end. "Okay. Try not to be too late. I don't want you burning yourself out at an early age. You know I need desperately for us to grow old together."

Donna always reiterated the same statement, and Louis found it to be endearing.

"Okay, honey. See you later," he responded.

Upon hanging up the phone, Donna stopped and thought to herself. She always wondered whether Louis actually had a poker game every Monday night or if he was seeing a mistress. She knew that they had a strong marriage and that they both loved one another deeply. But in today's world, one could never be sure. Deep down, however, she knew she was the love of his life.

She dismissed that fleeting thought and turned her attention back to the children. She had the responsibility of organizing the kids' activities for the evening. Donna was a little resentful of Louis in this area. Though she had the nanny available at her disposal, the two children were tough to handle. Donna always thought that she needed a third person to watch after the kids, attend to their constant needs, and make certain that they were safe. But that third person would not be Louis. He had his place in the world, and Donna gave him the adequate space that he required.

The limo pulled into the DUMBO section of Manhattan and soon arrived at the entrance of a condominium.

"Thanks, William. Pick me up at midnight."

"No problem, Mr. Bexton. I'll be here."

Louis exited the limo, nodded to the doorman, walked inside the building, and got on the elevator. He took it up to the twelfth floor. Then he walked to a door down the hallway and knocked.

Within seconds, the door opened and there stood Larry.

A smile spread across Louis' face. "Hey, Larry. How's it going?"

Larry smiled back. "Grand, Louis. Just grand!"

Larry was Louis' best friend from college. He worked as a podiatrist in Manhattan. He owned a lucrative practice that he had spent years of his life building. Larry was a single guy who lived the good life.

The usual suspects were sitting around the poker table. There was Gary, a dentist and good friend of Larry's; Steve, a real estate broker; and Aaron, a rabbi who officiate at a reformed Synagogue on the lower eastside. This was the temple that Louis' parents had gone to when he was growing up. A few years earlier, the rabbi there retired, and Aaron, the then-assistant rabbi, took over the congregation. Although Donna was Catholic, Louis was still a member there. He and Donna had decided to raise the children without any one affiliation They wanted the kids to have exposure to both religions.

Aaron had officiate at Louis and Donna's wedding, along with a priest that had known Donna's family for many years. Afterward, Louis became friendly with Aaron and they grew to have a mutual respect for one another. And as a result of this good friendship, Louis invited Aaron to the regular poker games.

The stakes of the game were usually quite high. They generally played either draw poker or Texas hold 'em. The pots could be pretty steep, and on a bad night a player could easily lose $50,000. This was a serious game; not for the faint of heart.

Eyeing all the other players, Louis' face lit up. "Hey there, guys. Are all of you prepared to lose? You might as well just give me $10,000 each and we can call it a night; then we don't have to go through the tortuous ritual of dealing, shuffling, and betting

All the guys shook their heads and chuckled. Within moments, they started playing.

Since the poker game was such a sacred event for Louis, he made sure to turn off his blackberry and beeper. This was a way for Louis to unwind. There were no interruptions and no deals transacted; just a good time with friends.

An hour into the game, Louis looked around the table at all his friends. Then he cleared his throat…

"Listen up, everyone," said Louis. "I've been thinking about my current status in life. I have been amazingly blessed with good fortune. My belief is that it is now time to make a difference in the world. Trading and wheeling and dealing across the globe has been extremely lucrative and has allowed me and my family to live a fantastic life, but there has to be more. I want to do something to make a difference in people's lives. I want what I do to be a life-changing experience for those who are the recipients of my good deeds."

Aaron chimed in immediately, with great passion: "Louis, my dear friend, there are many opportunities at the synagogue for you to participate in. I have been after you for a number of years to serve as the treasurer or chairman of the finance committee. With your business acumen and your financial background, you could help the temple reach the next level. We need to find a new home for the temple…or maybe just do a major renovation to the sanctuary and the building. With your contacts in the financial community and your business strategies, you could be extremely instrumental in obtaining the necessary financ ing for the building project."

Louis frowned for a moment before responding. "No offense, Aaron, but your proposal is really not something that I had in mind. I don't think that helping a group of rich Manhattan Jews fits into my definition of making a life-changing difference. As a matter of fact, I believe that it's all a bunch of horseshit. Let the congregation pony up some money for the expansion and be done with it."

Aaron's face fell in disappointment. He did not know what to say in response.

Then Larry chimed in. "Louis, how about donating your organs to science? That is one of the most charitable deeds that a person can do."

Louis sighed. "I've already done that. Besides I want to be able to live to see the *fruit* of my charitable endeavors."

"Well, you *could* donate an organ while you're still alive,"

Larry told him.

"That's true," Louis mumbled back, still not satisfied with his friends' suggestions.

After some more discussion, Louis realized that he was not going to get any new ideas from his poker buddies, so he maneuvered away from the topic. The conversation shifted to sports, and to focusing on the big blind and the little blind in exas hold 'em.

Since Louis not only had money, but balls as well, he was a force to be reckoned with. He won one hand with a pair of deuces. Two of the other players beat him with the cards, but not with the cerebral strength of hanging in there till the end. One had a set of nines and the other had a straight. And so, when Louis went all in with a pair of deuces, everyone went scrambling for safety and folded like cheap suits.

At around 10 pm, the guys took a break. Some of them mixed drinks. Louis called Donna to see how her night was going.

The rabbi, on the other hand, spent his break differently from the others.

The rabbi was in the corner snorting a double line of cocaine.

Aaron denied that he had a problem. Louis and the other guys never said anything to Aaron about his cocaine, as they didn't want to anger him. But Louis had always believed that the rabbi was headed toward a future meltdown.

Aaron had four beautiful children and a lovely wife. They lived in a brownstone in Greenwich Village. Aaron's wife had inherited the apartment from her parents. The family had no idea about Aaron's habit. In fact, he never even admitted to any of the guys that it *was* a habit. Instead, he maintained that he only snorted cocaine when he played poker. Aaron believed that the cocaine activated his brain and pushed him closer to God. And maybe there was some truth to this. After a couple snorts, he did tend to win more frequently.

But Louis was deeply concerned about Aaron. He believed this was more than a recreational endeavor. Louis was convinced that Aaron was addicted to cocaine and that it would soon destroy his life and his family's life, ruining his chances at continuing to practice as a rabbi.

But there was nothing he could do to get through to his friend.

Everyone went back to their designated seats around the table, and soon the game resumed.

Chapter Three

William was a loyal employee who was always there for his boss, Mr. Bexton. Not only was William positive and punctual, but he also listened when his boss was frustrated after a stressful day of work.

William was born and raised in South Philadelphia. He dropped out of LaSalle University and wound up in New York to pursue an acting career. To make ends meet, he filled the role of Mr. Bexton's reliable dri er.

After William dropped his boss off at the poker game, he looked at his watch and saw that he had a number of free hours to himself. He thought about his audition on Wednesday, and immediately, butterflie filled his stomach. He had played a number of small roles, had done many walk-ons and stand-in roles in various movies and commercials. But it wasn't enough. William was thirty-two years old, and he felt that his acting career was flounde-ing. It would only be a matter of time before his robust stature was diminished.

At times William was envious of Louis, a self-made multi-millionaire with a beautiful family and a great life. In some sense William was the complete antithesis of his boss. But where else was William going to earn $100,000, plus benefits, than working as the personal slave to a successful Wall Street trader?

Even though William was a college dropout with little to no assets, he was still treated fine by his boss. Also, in Louis' company, he never felt intimidated. William lived in a walk-up apartment in the neighborhood of Chelsea in NYC. He rented the one-bedroom for about $2,000 per month, plus utilities. He did not need to buy a car, as he either had the Bexton limo or another car available to him at no cost as part of his compensation arrangement with Mr. Bexton.

William drove slowly through the meatpacking district in downtown Manhattan. It was a Monday night, and things in the area were relatively quiet. He was looking for some action, knowing that he had several hours until the end of the poker game. But he had to remember the rule: No alcohol while driving. Mr. Bexton was firm about this rule, and William had been compliant from the beginning.

But there were no rules when it came to sex.

In that area, it was "anything goes," as long as William was on time for all his appointments with the Bextons.

William drove up to a neighborhood club. He pulled the limo up to the front door, got out, and handed the keys to the parking attendant.

The attendant's eyes lit up with recognition when he saw the limo driver. "Good evening, William. The action is slow inside tonight, but hopefully you'll get lucky. I saw a couple of hot prospects for you, and they were oozing with sex. If I was so inclined, I would have stopped parking the cars and fucked the brains out of one of 'em."

William nodded at the attendant. "Okay. Thanks for the heads-up. I don't have a lot of time. I have to pick up the boss man at midnight."

"You have protection? If not, I got some condoms in the valet booth."

"Nah. No thanks. You know me. I like to live on the edge. Besides, there are enough drugs on the market to keep everything at bay, including AIDS."

Both of them laughed.

"All right. It's up to you. Good luck."

With a nod, William turned and opened the door to the club.

Then he stepped into a smoke-filled room where people were dancing very closely to loud—*blaring*—music.

William noticed a lot of raw flesh and got an instant erection.

It was a great club. A place that had everything. Under these hot strobe lights, there was only one missing element: females.

William had known that he was gay since he was in junior high school. His parents and sister were always very understanding of the situation, and they provided him with support during his years as a teenager and a young adult. In all his dating years, William had not met anyone that he'd wanted to settl down with. And so, he lived the life of a free agent and explored the clubs of Manhattan in search of his dream relationship. Many times, though, he simply had one-night stands to satisfy his immediate appetite.

This club that William chose had private rooms available to the guests. Taking advantage of this luxury, William connected with a companion for the few hours that were remaining and left the club at 11:30pm—just in time to be at the condominium to pick up his boss.

The night was foggy, so William proceeded slowly toward the DUMBO section of Manhattan. He arrived early, as usual, and waited for his boss.

His thoughts were obtrusive. He could not expunge from his mind the dark, secret life that he led. He did not want to reveal his lifestyle to the Bextons for fear that they would not be accepting of its alternative nature. William could possibly lose his job, and that was not something that he was interested in risking.

Louis stepped outside and into the limo at exactly midnight. "Hi, William. How was your night?"

William gave his boss a tight smile. "Fine, Mr. Bexton. I went to a friend's house to watch the basketball game; nothing too exciting. How did the poker game go for you? Any luck?"

"I bluffed one hand with a pair of deuces and was lucky enough to leave as the winner," Louis boasted, a proud look on his face.

The limo sped away to the Upper East Side.

Louis was exhausted. And he grew even more exhausted at the thought of his day beginning again at 3:30 am. He would have less than three hours of sleep. He always thought about changing the game to Friday night, so that everyone could sleep in the next day. Sure, he had the energy now, but in the years to come, who knew how he would feel?

As he sat in the limo, Louis silently promised himself that he would get up in the morning and begin his quest toward making a major difference in the world. The thought of doing so took the edge off of his exhaustion, filling him with a new kind of energy.

William pulled the limo up to Louis' place.

Before exiting, Louis turned to his driver and said, "By the way, don't worry about picking me up tomorrow morning. I'm going to go into the offic a little later and…I think I'll take the train to absorb some of the local color. You know, get some insight into other cultures. That sort of thing."

William looked at his boss with big, round eyes. He couldn't believe what he was hearing. *His boss was going to take the train?* For a moment, he didn't know what to say. Then he quickly collected himself and responded, "Okay, sir. Then I'll pick you up at the office tomorrow ening."

"Yes. 6 pm."

"6 pm it shall be."

"Good night, William."

"Good night, Mr. Bexton."

Chapter Four

Intent upon taking the train, Louis arrived at the station at 8:15 am. He knew it would take at least one hour to get to his offic given the various connections along the way. After he boarded the train, he found a seat in the rear.

It was quite a huge step for a man so far-removed from the realities of poverty in his country. The train had a collection of people from all walks of life. There were people in suits, and some in shorts and t-shirts; others appeared to be homeless and perhaps living on the train. Witnessing the diversity was an awesome experience for Louis. The train was crowded, yet no one interacted with the person next to them. People were either reading, staring into space, or listening to something being emitted through their headsets.

Louis opened his Wall Street Journal and began perusing the condition of various markets. He received an email on his blackberry from a client and proceeded to conduct deals on the NYC subway.

While he worked, Louis noticed fi e young black boys on the train. They were playing catch and singing to the music coming out of their portable DVD player. It appeared as if they had no cares at all, as if they were free to do whatever they wanted.

One of the boys said to the other, "Hey, Louis, what would you do if someone gave you a million dollars?"

The boy named Louis grinned and shook his head. "That would never happen, so why bother even discussing the issue, man?"

His friend shrugged his shoulders. "You can dream, can't you?"

Louis was surprised that the boy had his name. He thought about how he and the younger Louis were so far apart on the economic spectrum. There was a very high probability that the younger Louis' dreams would be shattered by some event that was completely out of his control. Louis' thoughts were interrupted by another boy in the group…

"I know what I'd do with a million bucks. I'd get me and my fi e brothers and sisters a good education. So we'd have a chance to finally move out of the ghetto. Then I'd buy my parents a nice spot in Brooklyn, make sure that they had a comfortable retirement. And after I made sure my family was living real well, I'd take some of my money and contribute it to other families that are less fortunate than us. It'd be enough money to allow them to get a better start in life."

Louis could not believe his ears. Here was a young, poor kid who was fantasizing about giving to others. Louis could not comprehend the fact that this young kid had a better vision for making a difference in the world than he did. A burst of inspiration flooded Louis' head. In order to fulfill his dream, he needed to kick his plan for impacting the world into overdrive. Louis' mind started to race, and his expectations started reaching new heights.

The sight of the young kids from the ghetto truly touched him. They seemed so content with their existence, despite the fact that they did not know what a better life was. But they could dream about that better life; they could call it up in living color with their wild imaginations.

Statistically speaking, if these young boys could not rise above and leave the inner city, then they would not live to see their adulthood. The level of crime and violence in the inner cities dictated that some unhappy ending could very well indeed cross the paths of these young boys.

Louis now knew that he was going to make a difference

by giving money to poor inner-city people. But he just had to decide who he was going to give to, and how much he was going to give.

Louis arrived at his offic energized. He was excited that the idea was coming into form. It was now crystal clear to him. He saw the path to creating a major differ ence in the lives of other people.

Once he got to his desk, Louis excitedly called Donna. "Hi, honey! I finally ha e it."

"Have what, Louis?"

"I know what I'm going to do to make a difference."

"That's great, honey. What is it?"

"I'm going to give to the less fortunate."

"Okay. Sounds good. That's great."

After hanging up with his wife, Louis tried to start working, but he had difficult focusing on his daily wheeling and dealing. His mind was full of excitement over his new mission in life.

He was going to be known as a philanthropist that aided inner city people in rising above. He would provide them with the opportunity of achieving successful and prosperous lives for themselves.

Turning away from his work, Louis called his friend Aaron and told him about the idea. The rabbi was delighted with Louis' choice and felt that this was the epitome of good deeds. To be sure, the rabbi knew that Louis could have easily bought more Real Estate or increased his net worth through trading. But he was choosing another path. The path of a good and noble human being. It was something to be proud of.

Now Louis just needed to execute the plan.

At 6 pm, William picked Louis up in front of the offic building. Louis ran into the limo, as excited as a young child that just got his first hit at a little league baseball game.

"William, I finally have my vision. I'm going to give major amounts of money to less fortunate inner-city folks," Louis exclaimed.

"That's great. How are you going to deliver the funds? Fly a helicopter over the worst sections of the Bronx and drop hundred-dollar bills all over the streets?"

Louis thought to himself. "You know, that reminds me of a story that my uncle told me about a grand opening of a supermarket in East Patterson, New Jersey. Today, the area is called Elmwood Park. In the late 1950s, they dropped twenty-dollar bills from a helicopter onto the parking lot of the new supermarket. It turned out to be a violent event. Lots of people got hurt as they were trying to grab for the twenties. The police had to beef up their presence and a mass state of chaos ensued."

William shook his head. "So I guess *that* idea is out!"

Louis chuckled.

The limo finally arri ed at Louis' residence.

"Goodnight, William."

"Goodnight, Mr. Bexton. I'm happy that you figured out what you wanted to contribute in this life."

After William dropped Louis off at home, Louis quickly entered the apartment building and approached his wife, who was in the kitchen.

"Okay, I think I know exactly what I'm going to do," Louis told Donna.

"What is it?" she asked.

"I'm going to give one million dollars to fi e individuals."

Upon hearing this, Donna let her face drop. "Louis, have you lost your mind? I understand that we're well-positioned financially, but do you have to be so generous? I mean, you're talking about giving $5 million to people you don't even know."

"I thought you liked the idea of giving to those less fortunate."

"Honey, I'm not opposed to the idea. I'm just opposed to the amount. I think it's over the top. Why don't you consider something like $100,000 each?"

Trying to maintain her composure, Donna looked at her husband, waiting for an answer. Her mind started to flood o er with worry.

After all, what if Louis became ill or was very badly injured?

Under those circumstances, he probably would not be able to work at his current profession. That would put the family in a different position. They would have to live off their assets, with no income coming in. As it was, two-thirds of their assets were tied up in Real Estate. The fi e million that Louis was contemplating giving as a gift was a significant portion of the family's liquid assets. Donna was terribly concerned. And yet, she did not want to give the appearance of being selfish. She just wanted to be assured that their financial position would be solid, no matter what

Louis took a step closer to his wife and softened his voice. "Donna, the amount I give has to be an *unbelievable* amount, so that it'll have a major impact on the recipients. We're in a position to do this."

Donna looked into her husband's eyes. "I need some time to think about it some more."

"Okay. Take as much time as you need. But…can we talk for a second about the method of delivery for my gift? I want it to be unique and unprecedented," Louis told his wife, a faraway look in his eyes.

"Fine, okay. You have any ideas?"

"No. The problem is, I'm brain-locked over this part."

Donna pondered this for a moment before she asked, "Well, what gave you the idea to contribute the money in the first place?"

"Well…I was on the subway this morning, and I saw these poor black kids who…" Louis started.

"What?"

"That's it. Maybe I should just find out the names of the boys on the train and give *them* the money."

"That's a great idea."

"What I'll do is, I'll take the train each day until I find them."

Louis leaned over and gave his wife a big kiss on the lips.

Donna laughed, pulling away. "Louis, darling, you are indeed a man possessed."

Louis called William and told him that he would be taking the train to work each morning, and only needed a ride home for the next fi e working days.

Upon hearing this, William was elated. He had visions of staying out until the wee hours of the night and having his way with some young stallions.

And so, the next day, Louis got on the 8:15 train, hoping to see the young boys playing and listening to their music.

But they weren't there.

For several days, Louis continued to ride the train to work, but he was unable to track down the boys. He thought about placing an ad in the local paper and describing them to see if they would recognize themselves and respond.

But then he figured that thousands of kids would probably come forward, fittin the description of the ones that he'd seen on that day.

Thoughts turned in Louis' head.

I remember when I was a kid. I came from a relatively affluent family. I never knew what it was like to be in need. I certainly never rode the subways unless I had a specific destination.

The week came and went to no avail. Louis was disappointed and decided to stop riding the subway. He would have to try another route.

The next morning, when William pulled up in the limo, Louis suggested that they drive to the Bronx. He wanted to look through the neighborhood and take one last shot at locating the youths.

While they were driving through the neighborhood,

Louis could not believe the conditions that the people there were living in. He saw burned and gutted tenements—with families living inside of them. Most likely they were living in condemned buildings that had no running water or bathroom facilities. In places like these, rodents outnumbered humans.

The two men continued to ride through the worst parts of the Bronx. As they felt uncomfortable, they made sure to lock the car doors. They were flat-out afraid for their lives. It was a fear based on pure conditioning, which came directly from their backgrounds.

A form of discrimination, Louis thought.

After a good half-hour of driving around, William quickly glanced back at his boss. "Do you want to keep looking, Mr. Bexton?"

The look on Louis' face was one of defeat. "This whole thing's like pissing up a rope. We're not going to find them. I guess we can go to the office now.

"At least we tried, Mr. Bexton."

William turned the car around and started driving south toward the Wall Street area.

Deflated, Louis looked out the window…and saw something that made him perk up…

"Stop the car!" he exclaimed.

"What's going on, Mr. Bexton?"

"Please, William. Stop and pull over in front of the Goodwill store."

"Why? Some last-minute shopping for the kids' birthdays?"

"Don't be funny, William. Just pull over. Let's go."

William stopped the limo in front of the Goodwill Store, and all eyes on the street were fixed in their direction. The two men got out, and everyone looked them up and down. The surprised looks on their faces revealed what they were thinking.

Why are these rich white dudes going to Goodwill?

Has the stock market crashed?

Is today Armageddon?

William locked the car, and with quick strides, both men walked into the Goodwill. They were greeted by an attracti e, elderly black woman at the door.

"Are you lost?" the woman asked.

Louis grinned and shook his head. "No, ma'am. We're here to investigate a life-altering experience."

The woman frowned in confusion. "Excuse me?"

"What type of clientele do you have coming into your shop?"

The woman hesitated for a moment before answering. "Mostly local people from the neighborhood. I don't know if you had an opportunity to drive around. The unemployment rate in this immediate area is about forty fi e percent. There are a lot of drug addicts and alcoholics in this neighborhood. Many mothers and fathers have dreams for their children, but these dreams are just never going to happen. The reality is that they and their children will most likely never rise above and leave the neighborhood. Many of them are destined to be here from cradle to grave."

William looked over at his boss, wondering if he had lost his mind. This wealthy, powerful man was standing in a Goodwill store in one of the worst sections of the Bronx. And to top it all off, he was now starting a philosophical discussion with the store manager.

Louis made direct eye contact with the old lady. "Ma'am, are you certain that if I donated clothes to your organization, they would definitely get into the hands of people that really needed them?"

"Young man, there are not a lot of things that you can't guarantee in this world…but this however is something I can guarantee 100 percent. The clothes will definitely go to people who really need them," the old lady said, sincerity ringing through her voice.

"Okay. I'll see you in a few weeks with my contribution," Louis told her.

William now realized that his boss was going to make

a difference by contributing clothing to Goodwill. The driver could not help but imagining a homeless man walking into the Goodwill store, only to leave 10 minutes later with one of Louis' Armani suits, which retailed for $7,500.

Louis patted William on the shoulder. "We should go. I've already been late to work the past six days, and I don't want to lose my rainmaker status."

When he got to the office, Louis called his wife

"Hi, honey. It's me. Ask our aux pair to watch the kids tonight, and let's you and I go to dinner at Joe's."

"What's going on?" Donna asked

"I finally ha e my plan," Louis told her.

"Well, hopefully the amount has been lowered," Donna responded.

Louis merely chuckled before hanging up the phone.

Later that night, Donna arrived at the restaurant before her husband. She took a taxi there, since William was dropping Louis off right after work. Donna looked sensational. She was wearing a black dress, high heels, and black tightly woven stockings. She also had on a pearl necklace and her Cartier watch. Donna, at 42 years old, was still a head-turner. She had been that way ever since Louis met her when she was in her mid-twenties. She worked at keeping herself fit and used many facial creams to keep her skin clear and radiant. Right now, she looked absolutely stunning.

Donna took a seat at their usual booth in the corner of the elegant SOHO Italian spot. It was an upscale restaurant with dim lighting and the finest tablecloths. Its Zagat rating was sky-high.

Donna's eyes lit up when she saw her husband approaching the front entrance of the restaurant. And within seconds, in dashed Louis, her knight, her rock, her everything.

The two of them had a special relationship. Though they had been together for a long time, her heart still skipped a beat every time he entered a room. Louis was not terribly handsome, but he did have intriguing, rugged good looks. When they were together, they were like two teenagers. Donna always laughed at his jokes, finished his sentences, and shared his dreams, which were also her dreams. Louis loved to stare at her, to touch her, to smell her, and most especially, to hear the sound of her voice. They were both so fortunate to have wealth *and* love.

After giving his wife a quick peck on the lips, Louis sat down across from her. "Okay, so. Let me tell you my plan."

"Before you go any further, I just want to say that the amount you wish to give is exorbitant and terribly unnecessary. What would happen if you became ill and could not command the kind of money you're making now?"

"Sweetheart, I've made certain that everything is in order for you and the children. You don't have to worry. Just understand, this is my passion. The legacy I want to leave to future generations of the Bexton clan," Louis said, reaching out and grabbing his wife's hand.

Donna sighed softly. "Louis, I just want to make certain that you have thought this through and that there are no doubts in your mind. That this is really the path that you want to embark upon."

Louis paused a moment before saying, "I'm certain, Donna. This is what I want to do. This is my calling."

Donna looked deep into her husband's eyes and was surprised by all the passion and conviction she saw there. This made her break into a smile. "Okay then. I support you."

Louis squeezed his wife's hand, grateful for her words.

Before they could speak any further, a polished, upright waiter appeared at their table, ready to take their orders. He nodded at them in recognition. "Will it be the usual for Mr. and Mrs. Bexton tonight?"

The couple nodded. They never hesitated when it came to ordering their usual—a bottle of wine as a starter; then Sambuca and a rare steak for Louis, and a rack of lamb for his sweetheart.

When the waiter left the table, the two turned to look at one another again.

Louis took a breath. "Okay…I haven't shared my idea with anyone. I'm going to donate fi e of my best suits to the Goodwill on Gun Hill Road in the Bronx. In the pocket of each suit will be an invitation to a dinner to take place on August 1st."

Donna nodded her head, following her husband's every word. August 1st was the anniversary of the death of Louis' mother.

The funeral had been standing room only. Initially, it had looked as though some people would have to wait out in the hall, but in the end, they managed to squeeze everybody inside.

Louis, despite his numerous talents, was without a talent for public speaking. And yet, when it came time to honor his mother by way of a eulogy, he spoke with quiet, simple eloquence.

He spoke about what a good person his mother had been. He spoke about how many friends she had. He spoke about the smile that she always wore, whether it was at a social event or around the house.

But most of all, he spoke about what a giver she was.

For his whole life, Louis had known this about her. But never did he realize it as much as he did on the day of her funeral. Not when he was sitting on her lap as a boy, being read a story. Not when she'd picked him up, again and again, during his long, twisting road to success.

For at the funeral, spread liberally about the room, were prizes and certificates. All of them existed in reflection of the various charities that Mrs. Ida Bexton had been active in. Whenever she had any spare time—and she had more and more during her later years—she could be found at a soup kitchen, ladling soup for homeless men, women, and children, or at her local temple, serving homemade sweet breads to disadvantaged neighbors, or at the local library, reading classic literature to illiterate grown-ups.

In life, she had gotten recognition for such deeds.

In death, however, she got even more recognition.

Lewis was interested in leaving this world properly. He wanted people to speak well of him after he was gone. He didn't want to be known as a slick trader or a wealthy man, as much as being acknowledged for such things made him happy.

He wanted to be known as a good and giving soul.

Louis continued on. "The dinner will take place at this restaurant in the private room in the back. The invitation will read as follows…hold on…"

Louis pulled a piece of paper out of his pocket, started to read, "*'You are cordially invited to attend a dinner at Joe's Restaurant in Manhattan on August 1st, at 7:30 PM sharp. It is imperative that you attend, as this will be a life-altering experience for you. You are one of five individuals who have been selected to attend. There is no RSVP required. P.S. Bring your bank account information, as funds will be wired into your respective accounts.'*"

Louis put the piece of paper down and looked at his wife. It was obvious that he was giddy. His eyes were full of a raw energy that demanded to be noticed.

Donna could not help but laugh.

She had not seen her husband this way for years. At that moment, she felt a love for him that was stronger than ever. Although at the surface of her thoughts, she still thought that his grand gesture was too excessive, she knew deep down in her heart that eventually, as time wore on, she would have to get onboard with it.

After all, she didn't only love Louis because he was smart. Nor did she love him only because he was a good person.

She loved him, also, because he was extreme. Whereas most people turned the dial up to ten, Louis always found a way to turn it up to twenty. And even when the stakes looked too high—even when the decision at hand looked too foolish—in the end, Donna knew that she would follow Louis anywhere.

CHAPTER FIVE

The next day Louis woke up, unable to contain his excitement. He walked into his huge closet, where every article of clothing was color-coordinated, like in the Men's section of a department store.

He went to the rack and retrieved fi e of his most expensive Armani suits. The suits were immaculate. Louis always had his suits dry-cleaned after he wore them. He was obsessive-compulsive about his clothes and felt uncomfortable if his appearance was even the slightest bit out of place.

Adrenaline flowing through him, Louis sat down at the dining room table, opened the inner pocket of each suit, and placed the invitations inside. The envelope of the invitation took up an entire pocket. The envelopes were very rigid, almost as if they were made of cardboard. Louis wanted to make sure that the recipient of the suit would realize that there was something in the pocket. He very carefully sewed each pocket closed so that the envelopes would not slide out. Since Louis had been a boy scout as a young man, he had learned how to sew many years prior.

After he was finished with the sewing, he sat back and admired his handiwork.

He was ready.

Triumph awaits, he thought to himself.

He went downstairs and found William in the limo, waiting for him.

"Good morning, Mr. Bexton."

"Good morning, William."

William looked down and saw that Louis was carrying

a large plastic bag. "What do you have there?"

"Today's the day. Before we go to the office I have to make a stop at the Goodwill to drop off these clothes."

"Okay, Mr. Bexton. Consider it done."

The limo swirled down the street smoothly, like a knife through butter. Within twenty-fi e minutes they were at the Goodwill store in the Bronx. Louis got out of the limo and greeted the elderly woman he had seen on his previous visit.

"Ma'am, these are the Armani suits that I was discussing with you the other day. They are very special, and I want them to go to very special people."

"Well, there's no way I can guarantee that they will be special people, but I can guarantee they will be people who are in need."

"Okay, I understand," said Louis, handing her the plastic bag.

The lady started looking through it, and her eyes became as round as saucers. "Wow. These are amazing suits. Maybe I'll keep them and sell them on eBay. I could probably get at least $500 a piece...Only kidding! Thanks for these. Really."

"Of course," replied Louis.

"What size are they?"

"Forty-four long."

"Okay, great. I'll put them with the other suits."

The lady walked toward the suit rack but stopped in her tracks when—

She felt something in one of the pockets.

Her face filled with confusion and she turned back toward Louis. "There is something in the pocket that I think you left in error."

Louis chuckled. "No, I didn't leave it in error. It's just a personal note from me wishing the person that owns the suit next to have the same success that these suits have brought to me in my lifetime."

The lady nodded and thought about Louis' words for

a moment. Then she walked off to place the suits on the suit rack.

His work completed for the time being, Louis turned and left the store.

After the door shut behind him, the lady started eyeing the Armani suits.

She had to know what the note said.

She walked toward the rack of suits and took one of them off the rack. She laid it neatly on the table in the back of the store. Then she took out a pair of large scissors, ready to open the pocket and read what the fine gentleman had written. She opened the scissors wide, and her hands started trembling. She placed one of the blades under the thread that held the pocket tightly sealed.

She closed her eyes.

Then she let out a huge sigh.

She simply could not do it.

She had worked for this charitable organization for 35 years and was a trusted employee, dedicated and compassionate about her work. She had promised the fine gentleman that she would carry out his wishes.

And she was not about to go back on her word.

PART II: CHAPTER SIX

"Momma, what's for dinner?"

"I'm making your favorite tonight, darling. Turkey, mashed potatoes, corn, gravy, and salad."

"When will it be ready?"

"At 6 pm sharp."

"Okay. I'm going on a quick run outside. I'll be back in time to eat."

Autumn loved to run. She was able to dream while she ran.

She would run in the park near her home. Her mother would always tell her to make sure she had a cell phone, a container of mace, and a whistle that could be heard from three blocks away. Autumn kept all this paraphernalia in a small purse that she wrapped around her waist. However, she was well known in the neighborhood and was never afraid for her safety. Yet, since she wanted to please her mother, she took all these precautionary measures. There had been rapes and even murders in the neighborhood, so one could never be too safe.

Autumn was an attracti e 16-year-old; she was about 5'8" and had a beautiful complexion. She was very articulate and inquisitive. She had aspirations of being a successful attorney someday. Her ambitions were set on going to Yale undergraduate and Harvard Law. She had learned from her dad that presentation was very important and that you should always look, act, and speak your best at all times.

It was a beautiful spring day. The sky was clear and there were barely any clouds in sight. The temperature was in the upper 50s. Autumn was wearing her usual outfit—an all-black nylon jogging outfit that enhanced her already gorgeous figure. She wore a baggy sweatshirt over the outfit to tame the desires of the dirty old men in the neighborhood. It was great weather for jogging and dreaming.

Today Autumn was dreaming about her first day as a justice on the supreme court. Being the first black woman justice appointed to the court, she was extremely nervous. But the virtues that her parents had instilled in her since she was a little girl helped to calm her ner es.

"Be confident, be poised, say what you think, and to thine own self be true."

Blinking her eyes, young Autumn gave her mother a look. "What does that mean?"

Autumn's mother, Susan, laughed as she continued tucking in her daughter.

"What do you mean? Which part? I said a lot, sweetheart."

Settling in against her pillow, Autumn thought about it and said, "The last part."

"To thine own self be true?"

"Yes."

"That's Shakespeare, baby."

"Fine!" Autumn exclaimed, sounding impatient. "But what does it mean?"

"It means to always be yourself."

Now Autumn had more thinking to do. Her eyes seemed charged with energy as she considered what her mom had told her. "But, um, how do you know how to be yourself?"

Susan beamed down at her child, impressed by how bright she was. Her future would be excellent, if she was given half a chance.

"Well," said Susan, "you do the things you like."

"But how do you find out what you like?"

Susan smiled anew. "Well, you like chocolate ice cream, don't you?"

Autumn thought it over. "Yes."

"How do you know?"

"I don't know. I just do."

Susan tapped her baby girl through the blanket. "Correct! So just remember who you are."

Now Autumn smiled, seeming to like what she'd heard. "Does that mean I can have chocolate ice cream for breakfast?"

Shaking her head, Susan got up to leave. On her way out the door, she turned off the light and said, "I told you to be true. Not to be fat!"

Autumn cracked up laughing as her mother shut the door.

She had a euphoric feeling as she ran through the park. There was a wide smile on her face as her dream of being the member of the highest court played on in her head. On these runs she could be anything she wanted to be, and she knew that some day her dream would be a reality. She ran for about an hour and a half before returning home to her family's apartment.

She then ran up the stairs and was greeted by her always-smiling mother.

"Honey, dinner's ready. Go get your brother, and let's eat."

Autumn ran upstairs to find her brother, Robert. She burst into his room and saw that he was playing video games when he should have been studying.

"Robert, how are you ever going to rise above and leave the Bronx if all you do is play video games?"

Robert frowned at his older sister. "What's wrong with that? The world champion of video games makes over $300,000 a year. Dad and Mom would go ballistic if they heard you speak that way."

Autumn rolled her eyes. "Come on. Let's eat."

Autumn was a senior in one of the public high schools in

the Bronx. She believed in excellence, discipline, and hard work. The teenager was an honor student and proudly ran on the track team; she was also part of the school's thespian society. With all the work she was putting in, she was destined to obtain a scholarship at a very prestigious university. Her father had always instilled in her the value of doing well in school. He had high aspirations for her.

He wanted her to make something of her life and not be stuck in the Bronx like the thousands of other young women in the public schools. Many of them never went on to graduate high school, let alone attend college

"My child," her father, Maxwell, would say, "I don't have a formal education. I dropped out of school just after the eighth grade. I am now a doorman at one of the hotels in Manhatt n. I have been at this job for most of my adult life, but it is not the vision I have for my children. My children are going to study hard and move on to a higher plateau in their lives."

For now, Autumn worked a part-time job at a local grocery store. Most of her checks went to the family for living expenses. Many of the young boys in the neighborhood were interested in her, but she was only focused on her education. She had no time for boys at this juncture in her life. She envisioned that once she went to a top university, she would meet the man of her dreams.

Autumn's mom had only graduated from high school, and she suffered from severe diabetes. She had worked various jobs, on and off. Finally, she decided that she would clean houses in the fancy areas of Manhattan. The family got by with the two salaries coming in, but just barely. That was why Autumn had to contribute a large portion of her paycheck to the family funds. And that was why it was so important for Robert to concentrate on his studies; otherwise he would be stuck with no opportunities for the rest of his life.

Autumn loved her parents dearly. They were atten tive and caring. They also did their best to attend all their children's school events, and even went day-to-day without new clothes, just so their children could look presentable.

The three of them sat down at the table and began to devour the overflowing meal that sat before them. It was tantamount to a Thanksgiving feast.

The phone rang.

Susan went to pick it up. "Hello?'

On the other end, she heard an unfamiliar voice. "Hello, Mrs. Watson?"

"Yes?"

"This is Sergeant Graham. New York City Police Department, Manhattan division. Your husband was taken to the city hospital."

"Is he okay?"

"Ma'am. I would suggest that you get to the hospital immediately."

Her knees quivering, Susan dropped the phone. She became light-headed and had to grab the chair to stabilize herself. It was the shock of the call, coupled with her diabetes, that took hold of her.

Autumn and Robert ran to her side.

"Momma, what is it?" Autumn asked.

"It's Daddy. He was taken to the hospital. They didn't tell me anything else," Susan managed to mumble between cries.

Without hesitation, Autumn called their neighbor, Mrs. Cohen, and asked if she could drive them to the hospital. Mrs. Cohen told them to meet her out front in one minute. In a state of shock, the three of them went outside the apartment building to wait. Within moments, Mrs. Cohen appeared, and they all hopped into the car.

On the way to the hospital, Autumn clutched her mother's hand. She had never seen her mom so upset and wanted more than anything to take the pain away.

"Mom. I'm sure he's okay," Autumn said, trying to be strong.

Susan shook her head. "If he were fine, the police

office would have said so. And if you heard his tone…it just…sounded so ominous."

When they got to the hospital, they approached the front desk of the ER, where a young receptionist was sitting.

"I'm Susan Watson. My husband Maxwell was taken here. I need to see him, and I need to see him now," Susan said, trembling.

"Okay, Ma'am. I'll get the doctor for you."

Susan, Autumn, and Robert waited patiently for about ten minutes before the doctor arrived.

He spoke in a quiet tone. "Mrs. Watson, I'm Dr. Harrison. Your husband has had a major stroke and we are doing everything possible to stabilize him. At this point he is unconscious and not responding to touch."

"Is he going to be okay?" Susan asked, not quite sure if she wanted to hear the answer.

"Ma'am…it doesn't look good for your husband. He's very sick."

Tears filled Susan's e es. "Can I see him?"

The doctor nodded and gestured for Susan to follow.

Autumn grabbed her mom's hand. "Momma, I want to go with you to see Daddy."

Susan nodded at her daughter, then turned to look at Mrs. Cohen. "Would you mind staying with Robert while we're back there?"

Mrs. Cohen nodded. "Of course not."

As if they were walking through a fog, Susan and Autumn followed the doctor down the hall. Mother and daughter had their arms around each other, and they were sobbing, praying that the father and husband they knew would be okay.

Autumn did not want her father to leave the world now. She wanted to finish her symphony of life for him. She wanted him to see all of her accomplishments. To live to see her dreams turned into realities. But most of all she wanted her father to be there with his wisdom. He was her mentor and her friend. She did not want their warm relationship to end, but to grow stronger. She wanted his love to last forever.

It was too soon to lose him.

Mother and daughter walked into the room. They both gasped. Autumn started to sob uncontrollably. Her father was on a ventilator; his complexion was almost ashen and there were many tubes connected to his body.

Susan came to her husband's side and whispered to him. "Darling, please don't leave me now. We have many years of a good life ahead of us. I can't go on without you."

Afraid to approach her father, Autumn hovered in the doorway.

Susan turned to look at her daughter. "Autumn, there is no need for you to stay here. Go be with your brother. Tell Mrs. Cohen to take you both back home."

In a state of shock, Autumn left the room and headed back down the hallway. She tried to fight back her tears. She wanted to maintain her composure when she saw her brother.

In the hospital room, Mrs. Watson looked at Dr. Harrison and in a calm voice, asked, "What are the chances of my husband surviving?"

The doctor looked down at the ground for a moment before speaking. "Mrs. Watson, things look bleak right now, but you never know. The next twenty-four hours are very critical."

"Can I stay here with my husband?"

"Of course. I'll let the nurses know. I'll have them bring you a large reclining chair."

"Thank you, doctor."

Susan came close to Maxwell, held his hand, and stared at him. She did not move or utter a word. Just stared at her husband, hoping that he would have the strength to recover.

She knew that he was in bad shape, but they were a family of faith. And now was the time to turn toward their faith to help them get through this most difficult tim

Susan curled up on the reclining chair that the nurses had brought into the room. She could hear the beeping of the machines, which were indicative of her husband's pulse. She could also hear the swishing noise made by the ventilator. These noises were disturbing, but as long as they were present, it meant that her husband was alive; and that was fine by her

Susan drifted off in the chair. Minutes later, she was awakened by the sound of alarms. Nurses and doctors rushed into the room, frantically attending to her husband.

One of the nurses put a hand on Susan's shoulder. "Mrs. Watson, it's best that you leave now and let us attend to your husband."

She knew that he had taken a turn for the worst and it was now a matter of time. She went into the lobby and looked for the sign for the prayer room. Upon finding it, she entered the quiet area and prayed that her husband survive this terrible situation.

She then looked around for a minister to heal her spiritual wounds. At that moment, there was a Hindu priest in the room. And since Susan desperately needed comfort, now was not the time to be faith selective.

Quietly, trying to maintain her composure, Susan walked over to the priest. He was positioned toward the front of the room, his head bowing down in what appeared to be a deep state of meditation.

Susan hesitated, as she was not interested in interrupting his trance. On the other hand, it was a critical moment, and what was the likelihood of this priest snapping at her in a visible time of need?

Just as Susan reached out to touch the man's shoulder, he lifted his head up, then turned around to face her. His eyes looked slightly glassy, as if he had indeed just returned from a deep, long sleep.

He blinked and smiled. It was a genuinely happy smile, but was not without sensitivity, as clearly the man knew that women did not enter this room for casual purposes.

"How may I help you?" he asked Susan.

Susan found herself shaking her head, and then found tears spilling over her lower eyelashes. It was impossible for her to form any words. Even inside her mind, she was unsure of what she wanted to say.

She just needed help, and she needed it now.

Quickly, instinctively, the priest walked over to her and embraced her. "Sometimes words are not what we need," he said.

Susan understood this all too well. She nodded.

But then, surprisingly, she found herself able to speak. It was almost as though the priest's dismissal of words took some pressure off of her and enabled her to use them freely. She said, "My husband is my whole world. If I lose him..."

And again, as though they were never there to begin with, the words left her.

And again, the two of them hugged.

"The world is so dark at times," said the priest. "So much hardship comes to people, and we can only wonder what it means when that hardship comes to good people like you and your husband."

Using her palms, Susan wiped away her tears. "Do you have any idea why it can come to good people?"

Hearing this question, the priest could only shrug his shoulders. "Life seems to be a school of some kind. A test for all of us to undergo. We do not know the destination. We do not always know if we learned anything, or when we did, if we took away the right lesson. But we are made to keep on trying. And if dark days await you, then remember that that is what you are made to do...*keep on trying*."

After speaking with the priest, Susan left the prayer room. She went toward her husband's room and found the doctor pacing in front of the door. When he saw her, his eyes became glassy.

The doctor took a breath. "Mrs. Watson, I have sad

news. Your husband has passed. We tried everything humanly possible to no avail."

Everything around Susan grew hazy. She found herself consumed by a fog; a fog full of anguish and despair.

Gathering up all the strength inside her, she slowly opened her mouth. "Can I see my husband?"

The doctor nodded. "Of course."

Susan entered the hospital room and climbed into bed next to Max.

"Goodbye, my sweet man. Why did you have to be taken from me so early?

"I always knew that this day might come, but I prayed it would not. The time we've had together has been better," she paused to collect herself, "than any words can really say. You have filled my life with joy and hope. You have given me more than I ever felt deserving of. You taught me what it means to love, and in my heart, I will always love you, dear, sweet Max.

"I will love you forever. And I will miss you till the day I die."

She stayed in bed with him for a few minutes longer, then gave him one last hug. She removed his wedding ring and watch before she left the room. Her balance was off; she was dizzy and could not see clearly as the water from her eyes would not stop flowing

But she could not lose it now. She had to keep going.

She had to call Autumn.

One of the nurses directed her to a hospital phone, and she walked right to it.

Picked it up, dialed, and waited.

"Hello?"

It was Autumn.

"Hi, honey."

"Mom! How's Dad?"

"Um...Dad didn't make it, baby."

"What do you mean?"

"He's gone."

Autumn started to wail on the other end. *"Daddy... no...!"*

After hanging up the phone, Autumn told her brother of their father's passing, and he immediately started beating a pillow against the ground to release his emotions. Autumn just watched him, helpless, tears streaming down her cheeks.

Mrs. Cohen, who was staying at home with the children, left to pick Susan up from the hospital. When Susan came back, she was greeted by her two children, who were both crying. She pulled them both into a tight hug.

Burying her face into her mother's neck, Autumn said, "What are we going to do now that Daddy is gone? He was our rock. He was the guiding force in the house."

Susan pulled out of the hug and looked at her daughter. "Autumn, we're all in pain now, darling, but we must carry on in a way that would make your Daddy most proud."

Hearing these words, the kids reached for their mother again. They hugged and clung to each other for what seemed like an eternity. None of it seemed real at all.

The true friend that she was, Mrs. Cohen spent hours on the phone, contacting friends and relatives, informing them of Maxwell's passing.

Mrs. Cohen had been widowed a number of years before, so she knew the drill. She knew that she would have to be the one to make certain that the family was guided through this horrific event. But she also knew that Susan was a strong woman who would, no doubt, eventually get through this traumatic event. She had witnessed her strength during episodes when the children were ill, along with the time when Maxwell was out of work for several months. Through it all, Susan always seemed to weather the storm. And now she was about to undergo the biggest test of her life.

Susan knew that it was now her job to be the rock that her late husband was. And so, she summoned up all her courage, and proceeded to plan the upcoming funeral.

"Autumn, we need to think about how your dad is going to look at the wake. I know he'd want to look like a dignified, successful man…just the way we've known him for all these years. We need to make certain that he has a fine outfit, befitted for a man of his calib

"Okay," Autumn responded.

"Tomorrow, I want you to go to the department store and pick out one of the finest suits you can find," Susan told her, handing her daughter $250.

The money had been pulled from the family's emergency fund, which Maxwell himself had set aside. He was always prepared for any kind of situation. Litt e did he know that when he was putting the money aside, it would end up being used for him.

Since no one in the family was very hungry that night, they all decided to go to bed early. The devastation of their loss had wiped the energy clean out of them.

Susan saw Mrs. Cohen to the door. "Thank you, Mrs. Cohen. You are a wonderful neighbor and a special person. I hate to burden you with this huge task of helping to organize everything."

Mrs. Cohen shook her head, a warm smile on her face. "Don't be silly. I wouldn't have it any other way."

That night Autumn lay in bed, sobbing hysterically. The reality of never having her dad around again was beginning to set in. A dark feeling started to take over her insides. Eventually she was able to cry herself to sleep. But it was of no use. She woke up every fifteen minutes or so with a terrible longing in her heart.

The next morning, Autumn left the house early with the two hundred and $50 her mom had given her in her pocket. There was a Goodwill store that Autumn often passed during her jogs. She had remembered that they had nice men's suits hanging in the window.

And so, she headed to the Goodwill store. The elderly store clerk greeted her with a big, toothy grin. "Good morning. How may I help you?"

Autumn cleared her throat. "I'm looking for a suit for my dad."

"That's great. What's the occasion?"

Though Autumn tried, she could not utter a single word. She started to tremble, and tears formed in her eyes.

The clerk looked at the young girl with compassion. She put a hand on her shoulder. "It's okay, dear. Come on. Let's go pick out something nice."

The clerk brought Autumn over to the rack of Armani suits. After studying the suits closely, Autumn's eyes settled on a dark gray one. She pointed to it and looked at the clerk.

"I want the gray suit. How much is it?" Autumn asked.

"That's $75," the clerk told her.

Autumn took the suit and handed some dollar bills to the clerk. Just as she was about to turn and leave the store, the clerk stared straight at her with her soft eyes and said, "I'm sorry for your loss. May your family know no more sorrow."

Surprised that the clerk knew, Autumn looked down at the floor for a moment. Then she walked out of the store, carrying the Armani suit along with her.

On the walk home, she could barely suppress her tears. How could her father be gone? It just wasn't fair.

When she got home, she found her mother sitt ng on the couch in her nightgown. Mrs. Cohen was in the kitchen making pancakes and eggs. Seeing the neighbor there so early in the morning made Autumn's heart melt.

"Mrs. Cohen?"

"Yes, Autumn?"

"You're a true saint. My father was always thankful for your presence. He always considered you as part of the family. And you *are* a part of our family. We love you very much."

Mrs. Cohen's face filled with pride. "Why…thank you, Autumn. I love all of you, too."

Mrs. Cohen went back to cooking, while Susan stared at her daughter in complete shock. She was touched by her openness.

Stretching her arms out toward Autumn, Susan said, "Sweetheart, let me see the suit that you bought for your father."

Autumn walked closer to her mom and handed her the suit.

She watched as Susan examined the fine material.

"This is top quality. I've never seen a suit like this one… except in the movies," Susan exclaimed.

"I went to the Goodwill," Autumn told her. "It's like new. It must have been contributed by somebody rich."

"Well, it was an excellent choice," Susan said, as she reached out and lovingly rubbed her daughter's cheek.

After she finished cooking, Mrs. Cohen went to call Hugsby Funeral Parlor to make the arrangements. When she was finished with the conversation, she turned to Susan and Autumn. "The wake will be on Tuesday night."

Susan looked at her daughter. "Autumn, sweetheart, when you get a chance, could you bring the suit to Mr. Hugsby? Also, there's a bag with the shirt, tie, and shoes for him as well."

Autumn was grateful to have another duty. She needed to keep moving in order to distract herself from the pain that she felt inside.

She walked to the Hugsby funeral home, which was only about ten blocks from their apartment. When she entered, she was greeted by John Hugsby, the son of the owner. John was a tall man in his mid-twenties. He had blond hair and a ruddy complexion, and his shoulders were rounded. He was wearing a black suit and his bad breath permeated the entire room. You could see flakes of dandruff all over his suit collar and shoulders. Autumn thought to herself, *He is definitely the poster child for undertakers. Who else would do this kind of job?*

"Hi. I'm Autumn Watson, and I'm here to give you my daddy's clothes…uh…Mr. Maxwell Watson's clothes."

"Sorry about your loss, Ms. Watson. I knew your dad; he was well-respected in the community."

Autumn forced a smile. Then she handed John the clothes, turned on her heel, and left—glad to be out of the presence of one John Hugsby.

By the time Tuesday night arrived, everything was perfectly planned. Mrs. Cohen had done a wonderful job of notifying everyone and organizing the wake for the Watsons. Even though Mrs. Cohen was Jewish, she had many Christian friends and knew a lot about the Christian customs. She was a genuine caregiver.

At the head of the room, Maxwell Watson was laid out in the open coffin in the immaculat Armani suit.

The immaculate Armani suit that had the invitation of a lifetime tucked inside one of its pockets.

Yet no one knew, and no one would know. No one would know that the pocket contained a ticket for someone to exit the ghetto, to live a better life. It was going to be buried with Maxwell. It would not be discovered by Autumn, who might have been able to actually live her dream and transform her life. It would not be discovered by her mother, who might have been able to carve out a nice, comfortable existence for herself.

Once the casket closed and was lowered into the ground, these possibilities would be shut out completely. Never to be realized.

After the family and friends who had paid their respects left, John Hugsby came in and closed the casket. The only people left were Autumn, Robert, Susan, and Mrs. Cohen. They sat there, staring at the casket, hugging each other, continuing to grieve.

Tomorrow was the funeral. Maxwell Watson would be

eulogized by his friend and brothers and would be buried in the ground with a one-million-dollar dream that no member of his family would ever have the opportunity to taste.

The family stood around for a while and then turned to the door to leave, when—

"Autumn?"

Autumn turned around to see John standing there. He was holding a note in his hand.

"This morning when I was tailoring the suit for your father, I found this envelope in his pocket. It was addressed to 'someone special.' I imagine it's a private note that your dad left to the family. So here it is. Maybe you will read it when you have some quiet time."

John handed Autumn the envelope.

It was sealed, and its contents remained intact.

Chapter Seven

Ronald Lopez was born and raised in the South Bronx. He never really left the neighborhood until he enlisted in the army just after graduating from high school. Ronald fi -ured that he would enlist, and the army would pay for his education.

He was raised by his Aunt Lauris. His father left when he was about one year old, and his mother died of cancer when he was ten. His mother's sister, Lauris, who had never married, took the young Ronald in and raised him. She was his substitute mother *and* father, which was not an easy task.

Ronald was a great athlete who worked very hard in school. He had hoped that someday he would get a scholarship to a good college based on his athletic abilities. The only problem was that his dyslexia interfered with his ability to excel. So although he was able to graduate, he was not able to obtain the type of grades that were required for any kind of scholarship.

Ronald was eighteen years old. He was about six-foot-three and 200 pounds. He did not have one ounce of fat on him. He was built like an Adonis. The women in the neighborhood, young and old, all loved Ronald. He was in high demand. But he knew that he would have to stay focused on his future in order to succeed.

Until that day came, his aunt had a job as an offic manager with a local trucking company, and despite the long hours, she did a fabulous job of raising and nurturing Ronald.

Lauris was not happy with Ronald's choice to enlist,

even though she knew that, financially, it was the right thing to do.

Ronald did have a girlfriend who lived in the South Bronx; her name was Alexis Greene. She was a real knockout. A junior in high school, she had a body that was chiseled like that of a statue. She was, as Ronald often termed it, fla less. She was very sexy, and when they were together Ronald would always say that his rod was at attention, ready to serve. She was also a brilliant young woman who wanted to be a surgeon.

Alexis was not happy with Ronald's decision to serve in the army either, as she did not want him to put himself in harm's way. She knew that he had a passion to help his country. He wanted to be a part of the changing dynamics in the military; he believed that by being in the armed forces he could protect innocent citizens in the United States.

It was one week before Ronald had to go in for his army physical. He was spending a lot of time with Alexis during that period. They were in love and talked about what their future would look like—after he got out of the military. They knew that it was not going to be easy. They wanted to embark upon a path that many in the neighborhood before them had attempted; unfortunately, these people were not successful in maintaining their unions. The odds were stacked against the young couple. They wanted to leave the South Bronx; they yearned to rise above and be successful professionals living in the suburbs.

For the week prior to Ronald's physical, he was having intimate sex with Alexis around the clock. As they did not desire a baby, they were super careful. They wanted to live out their dreams as planned. They did not want one selfish act to derail their future

The week went by quickly and, soon enough, Ronald was on the subway to Manhattan, en route to taking his physical. He got there early, yet there were still about a hundred young men present and ready to serve. The master sergeant that was in charge was a real prick.

This too shall pass, Ronald thought to himself.

He knew that he was not going to be a lifetime military man, and therefore would not have to put up with obnoxious sergeants forever.

Ronald passed his physical and was given instructions to report to Camp Pendleton in ten days.

He was officially in.

Though this was what he wanted, he had mixed emotions about the whole thing.

Quite frankly, Ronald was still just a kid…and scared shitless!

But he knew that it was for the best. When he came out, Alexis would be waiting for him, and the government would gladly pay for his education. This would open up a myriad of other opportunities for Ronald.

There was a lot to be done in the next ten days, aside from having more sex with Alexis. Ronald had to go around the neighborhood and say goodbye to his friends. He wanted to make certain that his aunt was going to be okay during his absence. He made Alexis promise that she would look after Aunt Lauris for the two years that he was going to be away. During these two years, it was almost certain that Ronald was going to serve in Iraq. And the political dynamics of that war were something that he had mixed emotions about.

In no time, Ronald was called to serve in Iraq. While he was deployed, he was in constant communication with his aunt and girlfriend via email. He made sure to keep them posted on his whereabouts at all times.

Ronald carried a laptop and a hand-held PDA device with him most of the time. The PDA was required to receive information from the higher-ups about where to report and what the itinerary was. The PDA device included a built-in global positioning instrument that allowed others to track where he was located. He had a transmitter so that his comrades could find him if he was ever lost or held captive.

This device was a godsend to him. He could send and receive emails to and from any part of the globe. He also had access to the Internet and was able to keep up with world events, as well as Google information that he needed. This was the glamorous part of the war. (If there can be any glamour amid the atrocities of war.)

The reality of the Iraqi war was that it sucked being there. Here was this eighteen-year-old man thrust into harm's way, not knowing what could happen to him at any moment. The tension level among the troops was very high. Many of them were patriotic and wanted to serve. Many were opposed to the war, yet did not want to come off as unpatriotic. Some of them were intent upon proving that they weren't weak or any less of a man (or person).

Despite all the day-to-day stresses, Ronald had to keep hoping. Had to keep reminding himself that at the end of this horrific nightmare, there was a world of opportunities waiting for him. Opportunities that would be impossible without the experience he was getting in the army.

Ronald had a couple of buddies that he became close with during his stay in Iraq. He was in a brigade that was on the front lines, where there was no shortage of risk and danger. He and his friends would ride Humvees through various areas every morning to help watch over and protect the Iraqi citizens.

The heat in the Middle East was intense. And the heavy uniforms and equipment did not help matters. Occasionally a soldier would keel over from heat exhaustion; it was something that everyone had grown accustomed to witnessing.

Ronald was on a nine-month tour in Iraq, and based on his calculations, that was 273 days. He developed a ritual of keeping track of the days by placing tally marks on the cover of his laptop.

Since Ronald was doing a lot of physical labor in the army, he was losing weight and, on his way to having a svelte physique. One night he took a picture of himself completely naked and emailed the photo to Alexis. He wanted to see what her response would be.

Within a few hours, he received an email from her:

Wow, honey, you look great. You've lost a lot of weight! I wish you were here by my side so we could screw into the late night.

Ronald was immediately at attention. Now it was time to divert his mind and concentrate on other matters

He not only missed the closeness of her body, but it was hard to exist without that emotional connection that they shared.

However, he had no choice but to press on.

The command leader in Ronald's brigade was a twenty-six-year-old hotshot. He basked in the glory of his authority, always barking out commands to his men. He was the epitome of a control freak. Ronald was okay with the situation as he knew that it was only temporary.

Yes, temporary.

That was the only thing getting him through this ordeal.

On one clear morning, Ronald and his team were going on a routine delivery mission to bring supplies to one of the posts that was located in the middle of a combat area. The men were three to a vehicle, riding down a dirt road. This was a routine mission that the team had done many times before.

But something different happened this time. Something that was pretty far from routine.

There was an explosion in the road. With great force, it completely blew apart the vehicle that was at the front of the caravan.

Adrenaline pumped through the veins of all the men.

Ronald and two of his buddies took cover.

The commander yelled to everyone to get to the vehicle that was hit and provide support to the wounded men.

Ronald, a young man from the Bronx, had never seen

anything like this before. He was panic-stricken. He jumped out of his vehicle and went to aid his colleagues. When he arrived at the vehicle, it was a mess. Body parts and blood all over the place. Ronald saw that one of the men had the bottom half of his body severed from the rest of him. He was still alive—and begging for Ronald to stop the pain. Ronald started to tremble uncontrollably. He shit his pants, unable to move.

Nothing in the world could prepare a human being for this.

"Lopez!" the sergeant barked at Ronald. "Lopez! Get your ass in gear and provide assistance to these men!"

Ronald concentrated really hard to string his words together. "I can't, sir. I can't move."

"Lopez, move! And move now!"

Ronald slowly dragged himself to aid the poor guy.

Life for Ronald Lopez would never be the same.

As hard as Ronald tried, he could do nothing for this man. He watched as his poor comrade took one last, strained breath, his eyes going dim forever.

Ronald had been raising his hand for a full thirty seconds before his teacher, Mrs. Wilbur, finally turned around from the chalkboard, where she had been writing down the names of Civil War generals, and called on him: "Yes, Ronald?"

"Why is war, like, um, okay?"

Mrs. Wilbur wrinkled her eyebrows, drawing them close together. "What do you mean, Ronald? I don't follow you."

The other students were either staring ahead blankly or looking at Ronald with puzzled faces.

"I mean, don't we arrest people when they shoot each other?"

Clearing her throat, the teacher said, "Yes, Ronald, but in war it's different. The people who fight are part of the government."

"They're like...policemen?"

"Sort of. But they're soldiers. There's a difference."

"But um..."

Although Mrs. Wilbur didn't sigh, Ronald felt her frustration broiling just beneath the surface. Ronald did not always participate in class, but when he did, it was usually at the expense of the teacher's patience.

He continued, "Don't you tell us not to fight?"

"Of course! This is a school. Not a battlefield."

Some of the students covered their mouths and giggled.

Ronald looked around, a bit embarrassed. Still, though, his embarrassment was outweighed by his need to understand. "I just don't get how, like, all these guys in the battlefields shoot each other, and we just go around thinking it's normal."

"It is normal!" Mrs. Wilbur exclaimed, somewhere between angry and exasperated. "Ronald, there's a lot that you don't know about the way the world works. In this world, people have to fight. If we didn't have soldiers, we wouldn't be safe. If they didn't have soldiers back in The Civil War, ninety percent of the people in this room wouldn't be free! The best thing is for all people to be peaceful, but the unfortunate thing is that peace comes at a cost. And sometimes that cost isn't peaceful."

Although Ronald only grasped three-quarters or so of what was being said to him, he got the message on an intuitive level.

And he never, ever forgot it.

From the day of the violence onward, whenever Ronald went to bed, he would always have the sight of his friend torn apart and dying in front of him. He was never able to recover fully from the shock to his system. He could not remove that horrible vision from his thoughts. It was the same picture over and over. Nothing could divert these intrusions.

Ronald did his tour of duty and returned to the states. He felt that he was not allowed to discuss his feelings, as such was not the way in the United States Army. Men were men, and they had to learn how to deal with the situation, how to be strong and stoic.

Ronald became severely depressed and had to enter a

Veterans Hospital for treatment. The army had improved in their treatment of mental disorders, but they still had a long way to go.

Ronald was soon diagnosed with post-traumatic stress disorder and was given counseling one day per week on an outpatient basis.

Initially Alexis was supportive of him, and they tried to keep their unwavering love for one another strong. But as time went on, Ronald's disposition began to wear on Alexis. She was twenty years old and did not want to be burdened with Ronald's emotional problems at this stage in her life. She wanted to move on to another chapter. She knew that Ronald was very vulnerable at this point, and she did not want to put him over the edge. But she knew that she had to tell him her feelings (sooner, rather than later), so he knew where he stood. She struggled with this night and day. Yet her confidants all agreed that breaking up was the route to take.

One Thursday morning, about three months after Ronald returned from Iraq, Alexis met him and told him the truth. He was shocked. His whole life seemed to unravel before his very eyes.

He was already in such a fragile state, and now this?

This was a major blow to him, and from that point forward, the blue sunny skies always appeared black to him.

His life was in complete turmoil. He was depressed; he had no girlfriend and no job, and when he woke up in the morning, it seemed like it was ten o'clock at night. It was such a struggle for him to move forward.

Ronald's counseling appointment was every Wednesday at 10 am at the Veterans Hospital. He had to wait almost an entire week before his next appointment. His psychiatrist had said that if there was an emergency, he could call at any time. Ronald was not going to go down that path. As a good soldier, he was going to wait until his next appointment, in fi e more days.

His Aunt Lauris, whom he had moved back in with,

was a saint. She made sure that he kept his appointments, and she tried to do all that she could to lift his spirits.

"Ronald, dear, I think that I will go with you to your appointment on Wednesday."

"Aunt Lauris, you can't do that. That would be embarrassing. A grown man can't be taken to his doctor's appointment by his aunt. What am I? Three years old, going for my booster shots?"

"Ronald, sometimes people have different obstacles in their lives. And they're put in a position where they need help from their loved ones. Please, honey, let your aunt help you. Your mother would have wanted it that way."

But Ronald refused. He wanted to go to the appointment alone.

On Wednesday morning, he walked into the offic

"Good morning, I'm Ronald Lopez. Here to see Dr. Greenberg."

The receptionist smiled. "Have a seat. Someone will be out to see you momentarily."

Dr. Greenberg shared an offic with a group of other doctors that practiced an array of different specialties. Greenberg was the only shrink in the office He was a truly compassionate doctor who was interested in helping his patients get better. He wasn't motivated by the economic benefits of his profession. Ronald liked Dr. Greenberg's bedside manner, liked the way he sincerely devoted himself to the Hippocratic oath.

The nurse called Ronald's name, and he was escorted to a small modern offic in the back of the complex. The room was lined with windows, which gave it an uplifting vibe by allowing natural light to come in. Dr. Greenberg had several photos on his wall. A couple of them were photos of his great aunt and uncle, who were survivors of the holocaust. The doctor mainly stayed focused on the medical issues, but he did on occasion have a personal chat with Ronald.

"Good afternoon, Ronald. How are you feeling?"

"I feel like shit, Dr. Greenberg, but thanks for asking."

"What's happening with the bed-wetting lately?

"Still an issue. I'm a nineteen-year-old man, and I wet my bed. Pretty soon, I ll be wearing diapers."

"Listen, Ronald, this takes time. You had a very traumatic experience, but you still have many good years ahead of you. Your life has been derailed but remember: It is only temporary. How has your anxiety been?"

Only temporary? Something about that statement rung incredibly false to Ronald.

"I'm still having panic attacks, and I never know when they will occur. They sort of come out of nowhere, then POW—it's like the end of the world is rapidly approaching," Ronald replied, sighing.

"That is very common, and this too shall pass. Again, I can't impress enough on you that trauma affects everyone differently. Trust me, you will weather this storm. It just takes time."

Ronald nodded, wanting very badly to believe these words.

The doctor went on. "And one more question…how have your obsessions been?"

"I still have to check my house fifty times before I leave. I keep checking my oven to see if I turned it off. Even though I live with my aunt and she is basically the only one in the house that uses the oven, I constantly check it. I'm really fucked up, aren't I, doc?"

"You are not fucked up, Ronald. PTSD manifests itself in many different ways. All of your issues are treatable. The important thing to remember is that they can be controlled with the proper regimen of medication and therapy. Are you still taking the Inderal and Zoloft?"

"Yes, doctor, I am," Ronald replied.

"The Inderal isn't giving you any dizziness or light-headedness, is it?" the doctor inquired.

"No, it's not."

"Okay, I'm going to increase the dose. Now, if you

can, please keep a diary of how you feel on the increased dosage of medicine. Bring your diary to the next visit and we will go over it to see if we have to make any further adjustments."

The doctor scribbled something down on a piece of paper.

Ronald fidgeted in his seat for a moment.

The doctor looked up at him again. "Have you been feeling depressed?"

Have I been feeling depressed? Who the hell wouldn't be?

In his mind, Ronald started questioning the whole therapy concept.

"I'm a little down about my bedwetting. It's very embarrassing."

"Don't be embarrassed. Look, I want to try a new medicine for your bedwetting. It's a nasal spray that can really turn things around for you, in as little as one week. You know what? Let's chip away at one issue at a time. First let's concentrate on your bedwetting and get that under control. Next we'll work on your obsessive-compulsive behavior, and then finally your panic attacks

"That sounds like a plan. Thanks, doc."

"Okay, then. Let's make an appointment for next week. By then, your bedwetting will be resolved, and we can focus on putting your head on straight. Remember, Ronald, if you have a panic attack and can't seem to control it, you have my emergency phone number. I always get to my patients within ten minutes."

Ronald really liked Dr. Greenberg. He was thorough and efficient with no bullshit attached. Ronald felt very positive after the visit. The doctor had formulated a clear game plan, which made Ronald feel very encouraged. Perhaps there would be a cure for his maddening condition, after all.

Ronald left the offic and started walking home. He started to think about what it would be like to be normal again. What it would be like to have a girlfriend, have a job, and feel good about himself.

He so missed the intimacy. Alexis was his friend and his lover; she was *everything* to him.

Oh well, Ronald thought to himself. *She copped out when things got rough. That's not true love.*

Ronald passed by JCPenney and decided to walk into the store. He immediately went to the Men's Department and looked at suits. He thought that once he was better, he would have to start looking for a new job and would need a new suit for the interviewing process.

He tried on a couple of suits. The 44 longs fit him perfectly. A suit like the one he liked would set him back about $200. But he figured that his aunt would lend him the money until he was able to get back on his feet again.

What would he ever do without her generosity? And it wasn't just the money; it was the support and love that she provided.

Ronald walked down the aisles of the store, when all of a sudden, an aura of fear and darkness came over him.

He thought: *Holy shit, I'm dying.*

His heart was racing in his chest. He was sweating and having difficult swallowing. Dizziness swam through his head.

Was this a heart attack?

He could not breathe.

He tried to compose himself for fear of passing out. He struggled to get out of the store. He felt that death was imminent.

Could this be real or was it just a panic attack?

Ronald reached into his wallet for Dr. Greenberg's card. But he was unable to retrieve it right away, as his hands were trembling, and his vision was blurred.

Luckily, after some effort, he was able to grab the card.

He dialed the doctor's number and got his voicemail.

"Hello. Dr. Greenberg, it's Ronald Lopez...your crazy patient. I'm dying. You need to help me. I can't breathe."

Ronald hung up the phone.

Oh shit. Where is the doctor when I need him?

At this point, Ronald could *hear* the thumping in his chest. His breathing was more rapid, and his clothes were soaking wet. Ronald was certain that the end was near. He was sitting on a bench, and he saw a policeman on the corner. He started to walk toward the cop. He wanted to ask him to help get him to a hospital immediately.

But he decided against it and just started pacing endlessly back and forth. The people on the street just stared at him, and no one offered assistance

As he was pacing, his cell rang.

"Hello, Ronald. It's Dr. Greenberg."

"Oh, thank God. I am out of control. Nothing is helping me. I need immediate intervention before I die."

"Relax, Ronald. Where are you?"

"I'm in front of the JCPenney. About six blocks from your office

"I'm with a patient. We're in the process of winding down the visit and then I'll be right there. Ronald, you are not dying. You're having a classic panic attack. You need to focus on something. Say the words, 'Yes I can,' while envisioning yourself in a normal state."

Dr. Greenberg raced from his offic and was at Ronald's side within three minutes.

Ronald looked worn down. He was frightened, agitated, and very nervous.

Dr. Greenberg tried to talk him away from these feelings. "Ronald, listen to me: You're not going to die. You're having a classic panic attack. How long has it been since it started?"

"About ten minutes."

"And are you feeling better?"

"A little."

"Okay, look at me, Ronald. It's just a panic attack. And these things last no more than fifteen minutes," the doctor said warmly. "The important thing to remember is that you just have to get beyond the fifteen-minute threshold and then it will be smooth sailing after that point. After a while, you need to let the demons in and welcome them. The feeling will become more familiar and less threatening over time."

"Okay. I understand," Ronald replied in a quiet voice.

"Diversion is the key," continued the doctor. "Maybe put on some headphones, listen to your favorite tunes. Make a deliberate effort to focus on something else."

"All right."

"And please go to the pharmacy and get your new prescription for the increased dosage of Inderal. That should eradicate the panic attacks."

"Okay. Thanks, Doc."

"Okay, Ronald. I'll see you next week."

Ronald felt lucky to have such a concerned and compassionate doctor.

He walked home and was beginning to feel normal again. He was, however, exhausted from the day's events.

When he arrived home he went right to bed. His aunt came home from work and checked on him.

"Everything okay, sweetheart?"

"Yes, Aunt Lauris. Everything's fine.

Ronald slept for about eight hours. He got up around 3am. He awakened to the smell of urine…

He had wet his bed yet again.

He went through the usual routine of taking a fresh sheet out of his gym bag, wrapping the wet sheet in a plastic bag, and placing the wrapped sheet in his gym bag.

Ronald had covered his mattress with a plastic sheet to protect it from the dampness. He cleaned the plastic sheet with soap and water. Sprayed the room with disinfectant. Then placed the new sheet on the bed.

Ronald got back into bed and stared up at the ceiling. He felt as if he were regressing back to being a child again. The whole thing was so humiliating. And to think, this mess had been created because of his desire to better himself.

He was frustrated with his place in life. He started

hitting and punching the bed as hard as he could

After half a minute of that, he stopped.

"What a bunch of crap," Ronald mumbled to himself. "I'm a grown man with the plumbing of an infant. How am I going to meet a woman like this? Unless, of course, I find someone who doesn't mind me pissing all over her apartment."

Ronald got dressed and went into the kitchen to grab a quick bite to eat. He had a cup of coffee and a bagel with butter. Then he grabbed his gym bag and headed out of his aunt's place at about 5 am. He stopped at the twenty-four-hour laundromat to wash his sheet. He was praying for the day when he could stop putting quarters in a washing machine to erase the trail of his urinary dismay.

Ronald returned to the apartment after a couple of hours. When he entered, his aunt was getting ready to go to work.

"Ronald, have a nice day, sweetheart. Today will be better than esterday."

When his aunt left, he started his bizarre behavior of checking the oven to make sure it was off. He must have checked it about fifty times that morning

Ronald thought to himself that maybe he should become a home inspector, so he could marshal his oven-inspecting ritual into a profitable enterprise. He left the apartment and walked to the pharmacy, which was just a short distance from where he lived.

It was a beautiful spring day and the sky was clear. The air was crisp and there was a slight breeze blowing. The temperature was in the mid-eighties.

This was the type of day that would lift any person's spirits.

But to Ronald, it was still dark.

However, he did still feel encouraged by his discussions with Dr. Greenberg.

"Good afternoon, Mr. Becker. I need to get these prescriptions filled," Ronald told the friendly-faced pharmacist behind the counter.

"Do you want to wait or pick them up later? They should be ready in about thirty minutes."

"I'll wait," Ronald responded.

I have no place to go anyhow, Ronald thought to himself.

As a matter of fact, the only thing on his agenda was to get his medication.

Ronald took a seat in the tiny waiting area, grabbed a magazine, and waited. Burying his face in the magazine, he looked at the words but didn't really read anything. His mind was preoccupied. He was wondering how he was going to get out of this tangled web that enveloped his life. He looked up at the counter and started to stare at this lovely young woman who had come into the pharmacy. She was about twenty years old with long blonde hair, big breasts, and very, very long legs. She looked like a creature right out of Playboy Magazine. She placed her order and came to sit next to Ronald.

He immediately got aroused. He was relieved to see that he was still attracted to women and not men. He thought sarcastically to himself: *What a great catch I would be.*

He imagined starting up a conversation with the lovely young woman. It would go something like this:

"Hi, I'm Ronald, a bedwetting, compulsive recluse who has an interest in spending the rest of my life with you once I get beyond the onset of this current panic attack, which is enveloping my whole persona."

Instead of saying these words, Ronald just kept his head buried in the magazine. He thought to himself that a relationship was something for the future, once all the bullshit was behind him.

"Mr. Lopez, your prescriptions are ready."

One benefit of being a disabled vet was that his drugs were covered by the generous medical plan offered by the United States Government.

Ronald bought a bottle of water, grabbed his medicine,

and left. He went to the park and sat down on a bench. Then he took his scripts. He remembered the doctor saying that it could take a week before he saw the benefit of the new drugs. He took the bedwetting medicine—a nasal spray. He began to spray the dose up his nose. Passersby were looking at him rather strangely as the bottle was shaped more like an injection needle than a nose-spray container.

One week passed.

Then Ronald got up one morning and did not smell the urine.

He rubbed his hand on the sheet and it was dry. He looked at the clock and it was 7 am. He had slept for nine hours with no bedwetting

Ronald did not want to get too excited since he had been wetting the bed every night since he'd come home from Iraq. But he was pleased with himself and started to feel slightly more positive. He knew that his appointment with his doctor was the next day, and it would be nice to report that he'd had two dry days in a row.

Ronald left the apartment and went to his favorite bench at the park. He started to think about his future.

Maybe he would get his life back in order, after all.

Maybe he would be able to find a job

Maybe he could even pick up a chick like the blonde at the pharmacy…and have the energy to fuck her all night long.

He started to think differently. His spirits appeared to be lifted. Finally they were spiraling upward after a long, dry period of negativity.

He looked above and saw a bright sunlit sky with beautiful white clouds and no visible boundaries. He heard the birds chirping and the little children playing. Things looked different. The smells ere fuller, richer.

He was opening himself up to the outside world. The dark clouds were fading, and he felt a sense of purpose and motivation.

When he visited Dr. Greenberg the next day, the doctor

noticed a dramatic change in Ronald. He reiterated to Ronald that it was important that he stay on his meds to get the full benefit of the treatment

"Thanks, Doc. I'll see you next week."

"Hopefully you will have something exciting to report to me."

Ronald smiled. "My first task at hand, Dr. Greenberg, is to find a job, so I can support myself and not have to freeload off my aunt anymore.

"That sounds great, Ronald. Do it. And remember, Rome wasn't built in a day."

Ronald did not walk home. This time, *he ran home*. He ran up the stairs, opened the door of his apartment, and shouted, "Aunt Lauris! Aunt Lauris, are you home?"

She came out of the bedroom. "Is everything okay, sweetheart?"

"Yes. I just want you to know that I'm going to get a job. I'm going to the employment agency this week."

"Do you feel up to it?"

"Yeah, Aunt Lauris. I'm up for the challenge."

His aunt looked thrilled. "How are you going to dress for the interviews? You'll need a nice outfit.

"I saw a beautiful suit at JCPenney for $200."

"You're also going to need new shoes, a shirt, and a tie. And, you know, the timing is perfect. JCPenney is having a one-day sale on Wednesday. All the men's suits are 50% off," his Aunt Lauris said, pulling some cash out of her wallet. "Here is $200 in cash. That will cover all your costs, including a nice tie."

Grateful for the help, Ronald smiled at his aunt. "I will pay you back with money from my first paycheck.

The next day, Ronald walked down the street, on his way to JCPenney. He walked by the Goodwill store, along with a couple of other shops, before he arrived at the department store. He went in and found that the suit he liked was 50% off, just as his aunt had said it would be. So he was able to buy his entire outfit with the cash his aunt had given him.

Ronald was ready. His medication had made a dramatic change in his outlook on the world. Keeping busy was not a chore, but an adventure. He called the employment agency and made an appointment for the next day. That afternoon, Ronald worked to put together his resume. During his brief stay in the army he'd taken courses on computers, so he decided that would be the field that he would enter. He knew that he would have to enter any company as a trainee and work his way up. But that was okay with Ronald. The next morning, he woke up excited about his 11 am appointment.

He put on his new outfit, and when his aunt saw him, she said, "You look like a million bucks."

"Well, I feel like a million bucks."

Ronald entered the building where House and James was located. It was a local employment agency that had a good reputation for finding decent jobs for people in the neighborhood.

Ronald entered their office which was very clean and modern.

"Good morning," Ronald said to the receptionist, "I'm here to see Mr. Waxman."

"Who can I say is here?"

"Mr. Ronald Lopez."

"Okay, Mr. Lopez. Have a seat. Mr. Waxman will be right with you."

Ronald reached into his suit pocket to make certain that his resume was nicely tucked away.

Within a few minutes, Mr. Waxman, tall and upright, stepped out into the waiting area.

"Good morning, Mr. Lopez. I'm Steven Waxman."

"Nice to meet you," Ronald said, shaking his hand and rising from his seat.

"Follow me to one of the conference rooms."

When Ronald and Mr. Lopez got to the conference room, they both sat across from one another. Ronald pulled out his resume and slid it across the table toward Mr. Lopez.

"Ah, thank you. You came prepared," Mr. Waxman commented. He picked up the resume, started reading it over.

Ronald sat there, waiting patiently.

Mr. Waxman looked up from his reading. "I see that you were in the army and served in Iraq. I also see that you left after about eight months of duty. It says that you left on disability. Were you injured by shrapnel or something?"

Ronald shifted in his seat. "No, sir. I wasn't physically wounded."

"Then what did you mean, Ronald?"

"Well, sir, my mind was injured. I am suffering from post-traumatic stress disorder. But I'm doing well now that I'm taking my medication."

"Thank you for being so candid with me."

Ronald nodded at Mr. Waxman.

Mr. Waxman looked down at the resume again, then back at Ronald. "I also see that you had training in computers in the army. Can you expand on that a bit more?"

In a succinct and confident manner, Ronald laid out his skill set. When he was through, he could tell by the expression on Mr. Waxman's face that the man was impressed.

"Well, Ronald. You seem to be a bright, hard-working, and motivated person. We have an opening in the Information Technology department of one of our clients. They are an oven-manufacturing firm that is located about twenty minutes from where you live. And there's also good public transportation to get you there, if you need it."

"Sounds great," Ronald said.

"You have time to meet with the company personnel this Friday?"

"Yes, sir."

"Wonderful. And I'll be there as well to introduce you to the key people that you would be working with. We're doing a lot of work with them lately, so I'm often at their location. Hopefully, all parties will agree that you'd fit nicely into their organization. I'm confident that you would."

"Thank you, Mr. Waxman. It was a pleasure meeting you."

"Likewise."

Ronald thought about what it would be like to work for an oven factory. Considering he was obsessed with checking the oven constantly, he would probably love it. He'd be able to check thousands of ovens every day.

It could have been worse; he could have ended up working for a mattress factory

A skip in his step, Ronald let out a nice, long exhale. He couldn't believe that he had been received so well. It seemed that honesty actually was the best policy.

Ronald walked through the park, on his way home, and a thought suddenly cut into his mind: *Oh, shit. If Mr. Waxman is going to be there on Friday, I can't wear the same suit. That would show that I basically have only one good outfit.*

Later that night, Ronald was sitting at the dinner table, eating dinner with his aunt.

"How did your interview go?" she asked eagerly.

"It was great. On Friday, I'm going to meet with a manufacturing company for a position in their computer department. I have to call them to confirm the exact time.

"Wow, I'm impressed."

"Yeah, but there's one problem. I need another outfit.

"Ronald, you know I can't plunk down another $200 for your clothes."

"I know. Do you have any ideas?"

"Yes, actually. You know the Goodwill store around the corner?"

"Yeah."

"Well, the other day I noticed that they have some men's suits in the window. And they looked really nice."

"Okay. I'll check it out."

The next morning, Ronald got up, shaved, took a shower, and got dressed—all in about fifteen minutes

The ritual of the sheet-changing was history now. Ronald felt so liberated.

He was a man with a sense of purpose. A man with a destination.

He walked around the corner and entered the Goodwill store. He knew the woman that worked there as he had shopped there many times in the past.

"Good morning, Ronald!" chirped the old lady from behind the counter.

"Good morning, Ms. Wilkins. I'm looking for a suit. Can you help me find one?"

"Well, I have these beautiful Armani suits for $75 each, and they look like they would fit you. They're right over there, in the window."

Ronald looked and was delighted to find that they were all in his size—44 long.

"Do you have a place where I can try these on?" Ronald asked the woman.

The woman laughed. "What do you think this is? Bloomingdales? You've been in this store many times before, and you've never tried anything on."

"Okay…how about fifty?

"Sixty and it's yours."

"Deal."

Ronald took some crumpled bills out of his pocket. All he had was $58.

"Would $58 be okay?" asked Ronald.

"Okay, son."

"And can you throw a tie in with the package?"

"Now you're really pushing it," the old woman responded, shaking her head.

"Okay, I'm sorry. Just the suit is fine," Ronald replied.

The old woman looked directly into his eyes for a moment, then she sighed.

"Okay, you can have the tie too. Just don't tell anyone."

Ronald's eyes lit up with gratitude. "Thank you. This is all I have now, but after I find a job, I will make up the difference.

When Ronald got home, he tried the suit on, and it fit perfectly. He had never seen a suit like this one before. The tailoring and fabric were of unbelievable quality.

When Friday arrived, Ronald wanted to be early for his appointment, so he got up early. Again, he couldn't help but delighting in the fact that his bed-wetting days were long gone.

He went to put the resume in his coat pocket and noticed that the pocket was a bit tight. He did not have time to check what was in the pocket, so he decided he would open it when he was finished with his interview

Ronald took the #18 bus, and it dropped him off three blocks from the Oven Factory. Mr. Waxman, the gentleman from the employment agency, was waiting for him at the door. They walked inside together, and Ronald spent the next four hours at the company, meeting various employees. At the end of the interview, he was offered the job of Assistant Operations Manager, at a starting salary of $20,000 a year.

Without hesitation, Ronald accepted the offer, right there on the spot.

After leaving the office Ronald was on an absolute high.

He had a new job, new clothes, and a new outlook on life.

The only thing missing was female companionship.

He remembered the beautiful blonde that he'd seen at the pharmacy. At that time, he wasn't ready, but now he felt confident about approaching women. He hoped that he was not moving too fast inside, as he did not want his house of cards to crumble as quickly as it had been built.

Ronald went to the park and sat on his bench. He remembered the item that he had felt in his suit earlier in the day. He took out a small pocketknife and cut open the sealed pocket of the suit.

He pulled out the envelope. It read: *To a special person.*

Ronald looked around him. Considering there was no

one else on the bench, the envelope must have been referring to him. He opened up the invitation and read it. His body started to tremble. He started to take deep breaths. He could not believe what he had just read.

He put the note in his pocket and checked it repeatedly every thirty seconds to make sure it was still there. It was if he had a winning lottery ticket in that pocket. To test his luck even further, Ronald went to the pharmacy to see if the blonde woman was there.

She wasn't.

He gave the clerk his cell number and told him to call whenever the woman came back to the pharmacy. The pharmacy clerk said she came in every two weeks for her medication.

"I shouldn't tell you this, Ronald," the pharmacy clerk began, "as you may not want to get involved with her. The medications she comes in for are antidepressants. She suffers from an anxiety disorder. You would think a beautiful woman like her has it all together, but…you never know, I guess."

Ronald's heart started pumping super fast.

Maybe she is indeed my soul mate.

Part III: Chapter Eight

The air was breezy, the skies were crystal clear, and the temperature was in the mid-eighties. Everything around the immediate area was quiet. The only sounds one could hear were the singing of the sea gulls and the ever-present crashing of the waves against the beach.

This was how the Bextons spent their summers.

At the Hamptons.

The Hamptons were mystical to them. It was indeed a magical place, where the rich and famous had second, and sometimes *third,* homes. The privacy was well needed. It was a major improvement over the hustle-bustle of Manhattan

Every year, from the last week of June until Labor Day, the Hamptons were home to the Bexton family. Louis commuted to work every day during this time. Every Friday, he left the offic early, hopping on the Long Island Expressway by 1 pm.

The ride from downtown to the beach took about two and a half hours. The traffi during the summer was deplorable; it seemed like everyone on the planet was going to the beach on the weekends.

But the long, tiring ride was always worth it.

Once Louis arrived at the beach, he was totally relaxed. As soon as William pulled the limo into the driveway, Louis could feel the tension in his neck and forehead easing. He was immediately thrust into a meditative state.

Louis and Donna had purchased their place in the Hamptons about six years earlier. They had paid about $4 million for the 3,000 square-foot house. (In Hamptons terms, such could be considered a teardown.) Both Donna and Louis loved the house. It was built in the sixties but was remodeled and had a contemporary flair. And Donna had a way of warming up any living area.

What they loved most was the location. At the time they were looking to purchase, they had a preference to be directly on the dunes. But the properties they were looking at exceeded their budget by a factor of three. And they just didn't want to have a huge mortgage payment each month.

The house they chose was off the beach and had spectacular views of the water. They were paying, essentially, for the location. The value of the property in the Hamptons was all in the land value. The homes in the area were all magnificent, though.

William would stay at a guesthouse on the property during the weekends. He virtually stayed by himself and only mingled with the family when there was a special occasion or a chore to be done. Otherwise, the one-bedroom, one-bath guest house was sufficient It gave him the privacy that he needed. He was able to bring his male guests back to his quarters and have passionate, uninterrupted sex for many hours into the night. And he never disturbed any of the family members.

Louis loved to just sit out on the deck, smoke a cigar, and stare at the ocean.

It was an interesting experience, living on the beach. During the day, the views of the sun glistening on the water were spectacular. However, at night, the ocean was very dark, and looking out at it gave you the feeling of being alone. Sometimes you just stared into the pitch-black nothingness, and there was no sign of movement, no sign of any activity at all.

One Friday afternoon, Louis walked into the house following work, while William retired to the guesthouse.

"Hi, honey," Louis greeted his wife. "Where are the kids?"

"Napping," Donna responded.

Louis grabbed his wife and pressed her tightly against his own body. He became aroused immediately; his erection was nearly breaking through her skirt.

"How about a matinee?" Louis suggested in a soft tone.

Donna nodded.

The two of them ran upstairs to the master bedroom and began to rip each other's clothes off, like they were two wild animals. Both of them were completely naked within thirty seconds.

Louis stared at his gorgeous wife, admiring her for a moment. Taking in her long, soft hair. Her fair skin and her sculpted body.

Though Louis was average in looks, he believed that he was a stallion in bed, and more importantly, Donna believed it, too.

Donna laid on the bed, facing Louis, and he moved on top of her. He stuck his tongue deep in her mouth and French-kissed her for what seemed to be forever. Then he entered Donna's vagina softly, and she began to moan.

She whispered in Louis' ear, "Harder, honey. Fuck me harder."

Louis began to thrust wildly in and out of Donna for at least ten minutes. She wrapped her arms around his back and held on tightly as the two of them fucked like it was their last day on earth together.

The two came simultaneously and both started to laugh with pleasure.

"How was that, sweetheart?" Louis asked his wife.

"It was okay," Donna shrugged.

The two continued to laugh.

Louis put on his bathrobe, took a cigar out from his humidor, and went to the bar to get a drink. His favorite was Courvoisier, a spectacular cognac that had an immediate soothing effect on his system after the first tastin

He exited the bedroom to sit on a small porch just off the master bedroom. From the porch, he could see the ocean waves breaking on the beach. The location of the porch was set between the two direct oceanfront properties that were adjacent to his home.

Louis lit his cigar, placed his drink on a small table, and plopped himself down in a soft cushioned chair. He puffed on his cigar and just stared at the waves, not particularly thinking about anything concrete. He just let his mind drift blankly as he concentrated on the sound of the sea, with its rhythmic press against the ever-glistening sand.

Ah, the Hamptons. The quiet, the relaxation, the enjoyment.

This place was quite a contrast to the hectic pace of his day-to-day existence on Wall Street. Louis loved it here. He thought about someday retiring to the Hamptons and enjoying a laid-back lifestyle.

"Honey!" Donna called out. "Don't forget we're having dinner with the Berrengers tonight. They want to meet us at Charlie O's at 7:30 pm. I called Angela to watch the children."

It was now mid-afternoon, and Louis had plenty of time before he had to get ready for dinner. He liked being with the Berrengers. They were a couple from New Jersey who summered in the Hamptons as well. They lived about three miles from the ocean, which was deemed the poor section of the Hamptons. Larry Berrenger was an optometrist in Bergen County, New Jersey, who had a thriving practice. His wife, Judith, was a former teacher who was now a homemaker and looked after their three boys.

For the ten weeks that they were going to be in the Hamptons, Louis would be there full-time for four weeks, and then he would commute for the other six weeks, back and forth, to and from Manhattan.

Donna prepared the summer calendar. She had something on the calendar for every full day that Louis was going to be at the shore. Louis noticed that one of the days marked a camp musical song and dance routine to be performed by their oldest child. Louis remembered when his parents took the family on summer vacations in New York State, and he participated in the summer camp activities. His parents never missed his plays or sporting events.

"You were excellent!" Louis' mother screamed, hugging him as he stepped out of the auditorium, still wearing his cheap green frog costume.

Young Louis looked around, embarrassed. "What are you talking about?" he asked his mother. "I forgot two lines!"

Louis wasn't terribly broken up over the matter, as he'd remembered the lines after a moment of thought and managed to make the pauses seem convincing to the audience. But still, his mother was overreacting, it seemed.

"It's how you played it off that matters," his father said, reaching over and ruffling the little boy's hair.

"Exactly," Louis' mother nodded.

"Can we get hamburgers?" Louis asked, eager for them to get on with their normal lives and leave the excitement behind.

His parents laughed, enjoying the moment more than he possibly could. Putting their arms around their son, they walked him to their car beneath the setting sun.

Louis wanted to follow in his parents' footsteps when it came to raising his children. He wanted to be there for his kids and make certain he was an active participant in their numerous activities. He wanted to be an integral part of their lives.

His son was only playing a tree in the play, but to Louis, it was as if he had the lead role in a Broadway show. He was the proud dad. To instill confidence in his children was a main focus in his life.

Chapter Nine

While Reginald Barrister was playing softball with his friends, he noticed some unusual pain in his arm. It was sharp, and similar to no pain that he had ever experienced. But he went about his life and ignored the pain for a few days. Still, it did not get any better. He wondered: *What could the problem be?*

Reggie was a forty-year-old postal worker. He had graduated from a high school in the Bronx after being born and raised there. He lived in an apartment with his wife Lorett and their ten-year-old twin girls, Alicia and Stephanie. He had worked with the post offic since the first day after he graduated from high school. In about six months, it would be his twenty-fifth year of service, and he would be eligible for retirement if he wanted it.

But Reggie did not plan on retiring. He liked his work, and he kept in shape by having a walking route. What else would occupy his time? Boring days filled with silly errands? Thanks, but, *no thanks*.

Reggie was about six-foot-one and over 200 pounds. He had a dark full beard and piercing black eyes. He was very active in the community. He was a deacon at his church and a volunteer fireman. But most especially, he was a dedicated husband and dad.

The pain in Reggie's arm was intense, and Loretta persuaded him to go see their doctor. He made an appointment for Wednesday and took the day off from work. He went to their family doctor, even though he knew that the family doctor was going to ultimately send him to an orthopedic doctor to evaluate the pain.

"Good afternoon, Dr. Johnston."

"Good afternoon, Reggie. What seems to be the problem?"

"I've had this arm pain for the past few weeks and it's not going away. I've been taking Motrin on a pretty regular basis, but it doesn't seem to provide me with the necessary relief that I need," Reggie told the doctor.

"Where's the pain, exactly?"

"On the outside of my left arm."

The doctor was thinking it was a muscle, but Reggie was pointing to the bone on the outer part of his arm. The doctor probed at the area and Reggie nearly went through the roof. He had always prided himself on his level of pain tolerance, but this was unbearable.

"Easy."

"I think we need to get some x-rays to see what the source of your pain is. I don't know for sure, but it appears that it could be a bruised bone. Have you played any sports lately?"

"I play softball every Sunday morning."

"Do you remember banging your arm or injuring yourself in that area?"

"Not really."

"Okay, first things first: Make an appointment with the lab to take your x-rays and then make a follow-up visit to my offic three days later. By that time, the x-ray results should be in. I'm going to prescribe a stronger pain medicine in the meantime, and this should give you some relief."

Reggie left the offic a little concerned, as the doctor did not give him an immediate diagnosis. He called Loretta from his cell phone

"How did it go?" Loretta asked

"He gave me Percocet for the pain. And he wants me to get x-rays of my arm."

"What does he think it is? Nerves or muscle pain?"

"He really didn't say."

Reggie made an appointment with the radiology lab

for the next day. The woman took the x-rays immediately, and he was in and out within fifteen minutes

He called his doctor to schedule a follow-up visit in three days, as discussed. In the meantime, he skipped his usual Sunday morning softball game and hung out with his wife and kids.

Monday morning came quickly. The alarm went off at 4:40 am. Reggie had to be at the post offic by 6:30 am. He got out of bed quickly and went through his usual routine before leaving for the post office His walk was only about fifteen minutes

This morning, it was foggy and rainy, the type of weather that Reggie hated to be out delivering mail in. He preferred cool spring days with clear skies. Regardless, being out and about did beat being chained to a desk. Mobility was his mantra.

After a few hours of walking his route, Reggie had to go back to the post offic to pick up more letter for delivery. As he was walking back, his cell phone rang. He saw that the call came up as "unavailable."

"Hello?"

"Hello, Reggie, it's Dr. Johnston. We got everything back from the radiology lab."

"Is everything okay?"

"Well…one of the x-rays showed a lesion on your left arm. You need to come see me immediately. We will have to perform some further tests to determine what caused the lesion."

Reggie started to feel the color rushing out of his face. A feeling of nausea slammed into him. He had expected to be told to take it easy, and that his pain would heal in no time.

"Okay. I'll be there. Bye."

Reggie felt like he was going to pass out. His head was swimming. He did not like the tone of the doctor's voice. He sounded concerned…as if something serious was going on.

Reggie got on the phone and called his wife. "Honey, the doctor said I had a lesion on the bone on my left arm, and that I need to see him now."

Loretta as quiet for a moment, and then—

"Okay. I'll get Mrs. Wagner to watch the girls and then I'll meet you at the doctor's office

Reggie dropped off his bag of mail at the post offic and told his supervisor that he had another doctor's appointment.

"Everything okay, Reg?" asked the supervisor.

"Yeah, everything is fine. It's just part of my annual check- up."

"See you tomorrow, then."

"Right. Tomorrow."

The worst possible scenarios started running through

Reggie's mind. His dad died of cancer in his fifties, and Reggie worried that maybe he was following down that path at a much younger age.

Jimmy Barrister hadn't spoken in several hours, but when he finally opened his mouth, he spoke without slowness or muddiness or any detectable lack of clarity: "Bring me Reginald," he said.

And so his little niece, Cynthia, who was only nine years old, had no choice but to run out into the hallway and fetch her cousin, Reggie. The relatives had been taking turns attending to Jimmy's hospital bed, and the past half hour had been little Cynthia's turn. Happy to be getting a break, she escorted little Reggie inside and ran back out into the hallway, no doubt to pound the buttons on the soda machine out there.

"Son," said Jimmy, "come on over here."

Jimmy wagged a hard, crusty finger toward himself, and Reggie, who had always been somewhat frightened of the old man, dutifully stepped over to him and stood at attention, like a soldier awaiting orders from a commander.

"I want you to take a good hard look at me," the old man said.

He wasn't kidding around. This was a man with tumors all over his liver, gall bladder, and lower intestine. He'd never been a fan of doctors, and they hadn't detected the cancer until it had done a major job of tearing his insides to pieces.

Reggie looked at his father, exactly as he'd been told to.

"You live a good life, okay? You find love. You find a woman to love you, and one you enjoy loving back. 'Cause the rest of it is all fucking bullshit. Your career. Your reputation. Whether or not people like you. None of that matters one damn lick. It's what's in here..." Jimmy patted his heart through his breastplate... "that matters. And you fill it up. You hear me? You fill it up."

The old man's tone had been harsh and flat, almost as though he was reprimanding young Reggie. Reggie wondered then—and would continue to wonder for the rest of his life—whether his dad had ever found the love that he was saying was so important.

Reggie tried to be positive. But he could not help thinking about how gravely serious the doctor's tone had been.

Reggie met Loretta in the lobby of the building and together they went up to the doctor's office

"Reggie, honey, everything is going to be fine," Loretta told him. "You know these doctors. They have to cover all the bases and run all the tests to eliminate all possibilities. And there is nothing wrong with going to a physician that is thorough."

The two of them waited nervously in the waiting area. Fifteen minutes passed, at which point…

"Mr. Reginald Johnston!" the nurse called out.

Reggie and Loretta followed the nurse down the hallway and into the examining room. There, she took Reggie's blood pressure and weight.

"Nurse, have you seen the x-rays? Is this something serious?"

Reggie asked.

"I haven't looked at the x-rays, but the doctor will be here in a few minutes to discuss everything with you and your wife. I mean, I presume this lovely woman is your wife?"

Loretta smiled. " es, his wife of ten years."

Smiling, the nurse departed.

Dr. Johnston entered the examining room and wasted no time in getting right down to business: "The x-rays showed that you have what appears to be a lytic lesion on the long bone in your left arm."

"What is that?" asked Reggie, as he started to tremble.

"A lytic lesion can be associated with multiple myeloma or certain types of leukemia."

"Holy shit. Am I dying?"

"Let's not jump the gun. We need to do a whole bunch of tests to make the proper diagnosis. First, we will need to do a CAT scan of that area. Next, we will have to perform a complete skeletal survey of every bone in your body to see if you have any other lytic lesions anywhere else. Then we are going to have to do many blood tests, a twenty-four-hour urine test, and finally, we will have to do a bone marrow aspiration and biopsy to rule out other factors."

"Is whatever I have terminal?"

"Mr. Barrister: No diagnosis has been made yet. Let's remain optimistic, okay?"

Reggie and Loretta just looked at one another, not saying a word.

The doctor continued on, "I'm going to refer you to Dr. Kleuth, a hematologist at the Luke Center. He specializes in diseases of the bone and skeletal system. He and I spoke, and he recommended the various tests. When the results are back, you have to sit with him for the complete diagnosis."

Reggie could see the doctor's mouth moving, but he was not hearing the words clearly. He was in a fog.

His worst nightmare had surfaced.

He was going to die a young man, just as his dad had so many years before.

But Loretta remained positive. She had her concerns, too, but she had to be strong for her husband.

When they left the office she told Reggie, "The doctor is just ordering these tests to cover his behind. Believe me, everything is fine. You feel fine, and you are fine. You look terrific as ell, sweetheart."

Regardless, Reggie walked around in a perpetual fog after hearing the news from the doctor. He had always considered himself healthy, and at his last physical, he had received a clean bill of health.

After hearing the bad news, Reggie immediately got to work. He spent a good portion of his time on the Internet searching for all the information he could find on multiple myeloma or plasma cell leukemia. He was a man possessed. The only challenge was that the Internet did not have the most current data posted—and some of the data that was present was very gloomy.

For example, according to what he read, if he was in the later stages of multiple myeloma, then at best he had six months to live.

Loretta kept telling him that there was nothing to worry about, and that the lesion was just an isolated incident that could be treated or cured.

Reggie was skeptical, however. He was becoming depressed and stopped thinking of his life in the long-term.

One afternoon, they went to a friend's home and the topic of retirement came up. Everyone was talking about how they couldn't wait to retire, about what they wouldn't give to have a dream retirement.

One man beamed with passion as he said, "Oh, I just cannot wait. This whole body of mine is rundown. I've got bad knees. I've got the recurring ulcer in my esophagus. And all that comes from the nonstop stress. They don't call it a 'grind' for nothing. So when I retire, I plan to move slowly. Not travel the world but travel the space inside my own skin. Get comfortable with myself. 'Cause me and myself have lots of catching up to do!"

Everyone laughed, until a woman chimed in and said, "Oh, that's not for me. I'd prefer to travel the world. China, France, Australia—all the places I've always dreamed of seeing. And to walk those lands secure in the knowledge that I've got no other place to be. No offic waiting for me. No boss getting stressed because I'm gone. Just the freedom to go wherever I please, and with whomever I please!"

Everybody nodded and smiled. Reggie, on the other hand, was thinking that he was going to be dead in six short months. Sitting there, he thought that he would gladly trade retirement for three more decades of hard work. After all, what he did wasn't slave labor; it wasn't such a bad vocation. He could keep it going, give it the needed hours. If, of course, the good Lord had mercy on him and let him live.

One night, Reggie was sitting in his work area, continuing his Internet search for more information on his potential diseases.

Loretta walked in. When she saw what he was doing, she frowned.

"Honey, you can't be searching the Internet constantly. Let's go out to the mall. We can walk around, grab a quick bite."

"Okay, sweetheart."

"I'll get the girls."

"Okay."

Reginald wanted very badly to feel elated, but instead, he felt dark inside. He was lethargic, and his thoughts were possessed by his potentially fatal disease and the battery of tests that he would soon be facing

The family did not have a car. They used a taxi when they were going on local trips. They had to rent a car when they were going on a trip that was some distance from their home. When they visited Loretta's folks in Red Bank, New Jersey, they would usually rent a car, or sometimes they would take the train from Penn Station in New York City.

When they hopped out of the taxi and arrived at the mall, Loretta and the girls were ecstatic. They were eager to do some serious shopping. Reggie went through the motions, acting as if he was enjoying himself, but his mind was fixated on his health status. Lately, he would wake up in the middle of the night, shaking and drenched in sweat. This was all too much to bear.

They all walked into a two-level bookstore. Loretta and the girls immediately went to the magazine section. Reggie, on the other hand, went to the health and reference section, which was on the second floor, where his wife and daughters could not see him. He started to peruse books about cancer and leukemia. In one of the books, he read a section on myeloma. When he was through reading, there were tears in his eyes. He also got very nauseous—something he could have tolerated…if everything inside of him was fine.

He knew for sure that this was the end. There was no doubt in his mind.

After a nice day at the mall, the family arrived home. The girls went to the computer, and Reggie sat on a chair and read the paper. Loretta went to the kitchen to prepare dinner. It was as if everyone had their assigned locations in the house.

As Reggie read his paper, he had his mind fixated on the Internet. He was waiting anxiously for the girls to leave it alone and go do their homework.

Reggie was the type of individual who generally kept things close to the vest. He did not share his thoughts with many people. Loretta always said that he kept things bottled up inside. He had one best friend, Arnold, and he was close to his brother, Richard. But he was not going to tell anyone what was going on until the diagnosis was made. He did not want people to feel sorry for him, nor did he want a constant stream of questions coming at him.

Loretta, on the other hand, was an open book. She opened her kimono to the world. She liked to talk about everything with her circle of friends and her two sisters.

Above all, as Reggie had said many times, "There are no secrets in our household."

Loretta felt it was good to talk to others in order to solicit varying opinions and get access to different points of view.

Reggie went to sleep early that night. Before retiring, he put together his To Do list, which revolved around the battery of tests he would be undergoing

When he arrived at work early on Monday morning, he told his supervisor about the upcoming tests.

"Is everything okay, Reggie?"

"Something came out negative in one of my tests, and they need to do more tests to eliminate anything serious," he responded.

Reggie's supervisor had trouble masking his emotion. Though he did not cry, or do anything dramatic, he allowed a great sadness to beam from his eyes. Reggie was not only a valued employee, but also something of a friend—or at least a very good acquaintance.

The supervisor, Mr. Jennings, was not known for giving pep talks or being very verbally supportive. More often than not, his good nature showed itself in more subtle ways, from giving bigger-than-expected Christmas bonuses to commending the employees casually in front of customers. But now, today, faced with Reggie's predicament, he had to force himself to be more demonstrative than usual.

"You know what I like to read about, Reggie?"

For a moment, the sadness actually left Reggie's face. Not that he became happy, but he couldn't help but looked confused. Where was Mr. Jennings going with this? Certainly the last thing Reggie wanted to talk about was their reading interests.

Regardless, by force of habit, Reggie found himself being courteous to the boss: "No. No, I don't, actually."

"Quantum physics," Mr. Jennings replied.

Now Reggie didn't know whether to laugh or scream. He didn't know a thing about quantum physics, and even if he did, he was reasonably sure that now was not the time to talk about it.

Accordingly, Reggie just stood there, staring and saying nothing.

Mr. Jennings tried to break the awkwardness by clearing his throat. "I bring it up," he said, "because if you know the laws of physics, you know that everything in the universe is connected. We are all part of each other, inside and out..."

Reggie did his best to listen, but he couldn't help but feel that his supervisor was dishing out voodoo, plain and simple.

"That means our minds aren't only in our bodies, but our bodies are in our minds."

Reggie's eyebrows shot up. "Say what now?"

Mr. Jennings smiled. "Your body is just a large storm of particles, all spinning and moving extremely fast. And your mind has the ability to interact with those particles, and actually manipulate them."

"Are you saying I can cure myself?" asked Reggie.

Mr. Jennings nodded. "That's exactly what I'm saying. And more importantly, I'm saying not to listen to any of those silly doctors. Because as much as they know, they don't know the whole truth. No one does."

Reggie nodded back. He certainly agreed with the part about doctors not knowing everything. As for all that other stuff, it seemed like an interesting topic for a science fiction book club, but he had significant doubts about his ability to move his cells and particles around with his mind. If something like that was possible, then why weren't people in need attracting millions of dollars?

Reginald had to take time off on Monday afternoon to call the doctor's offic and make all of his appointments. He managed to schedule everything for during the week, with the exception of the twenty-four-hour urine test. He felt that he should save that for the weekend, as he would be home and it would be more practical.

The blood tests and the skeletal bone survey were routine. That Friday, he was scheduled for the bone marrow aspiration and biopsy. Thursday night, he was on the Internet, reviewing the procedure. He became so familiar with it that he probably could have performed it himself.

He had to take Friday off from the post office Loretta joined him for the biopsy, to give him moral support. Reggie was extremely anxious. The test would reveal everything about his blood plasma and bone marrow. If there was anything wrong, it would show up in the biopsy.

The test itself was uncomfortable. The doctor placed about a 10-inch needle in his hip for the bone marrow aspirate; a small sample of the hip bone was taken for further microscopic examination. It was a good thing that he'd had lots of Lidocaine first. The nurses had him rest for one hour before he left. The entire time, Reggie was fixated on his imminent death.

The doctors told him that they would give him the news about the test results as they came in. The bone survey, blood, and urine would take about a week, whereas the biopsy would call for two weeks.

Reggie knew that the following week was safe, as none of the test results would be in. Therefore, during the next seven days, he would try to consider himself healthy. He felt a little lift in his spirit, knowing that he would not have to talk to any medical professionals for that single week.

When the weekend came, Reggie took the girls for a walk to the park. It was a windy day, and they brought a kite to fly

"Daddy, look at how high the kite is blowing!"

"Look at how fast it's whirling!"

Reggie felt like a kid while running with his daughters, faster and faster, as the kite flew higher into the beautiful, open sky. But that joyful feeling was fleeting. Evening was approaching, and Reggie knew that he would be getting his medical tests on Monday. A feeling of darkness dimmed his spirits.

Reggie and Loretta were up early on Monday morning.

"Do you want me to call the doctor's office? Loretta asked her husband, trying to be helpful.

"No. I'll call in a bit."

As Reggie walked his mail route, he checked for voicemail every fifteen minutes or so. Finally, at about 2 pm, there was a voicemail. It took about an hour before he had the courage to check it. When he finally did, he discovered it was from Loretta. She wanted to know if he had heard anything from the doctor.

Reggie called her back and told her that there had been no word.

"Then why don't you call them, Reggie?"

"I will, honey."

After getting off the phone with his wife, Reggie called the doctor's office and one of the nurses answered. He hung up immediately. He did not have the courage to speak to them, as he did not want to face the life-threatening news. For as long as he could, he preferred to play out the conversation in his head…

He visualized the nurse calling and saying, "Mr. Barrister, we have great news for you. All your test results are normal. You're in excellent health."

But then, in the next moment, he'd realize that he already had one lytic lesion. So even if the offic were to tell him that the results were positive, they would still most likely have to start immediate treatment.

Reggie knew that the offic closed at 4pm. After his shift ended at the post office he worked up the courage to call again. He got their answering machine, so he left a message…

"Hi, this is Reginald Barrister. This message is for Barbara. I was wondering if she had my lab test results. If yes, could she please leave the information on my cell? I will be traveling on Tuesday, so the cell is the only manner in which I can be reached. Thanks."

It was a lie, but it relieved him of having to hold a conversation in his present frame of mind.

That Monday was host to another sleepless night. Good or bad, he needed a resolution, and he needed it soon. Otherwise, he was going to go absolutely mad.

When Tuesday arrived, he knew that there was a ninety percent chance that the results would finally be ready

And he was right.

At 11am, he saw there was a voicemail.

But he did not check the message until two o'clock.

In between, he received two calls from Loretta wanting to know what was going on. He assured her that he would get the information and let her know what was going on soon.

When he finally checked the message, he found that it was from the nurse. In the voicemail, she told him to call the offic and speak to the doctor about some of the test results, which came back positive.

Reggie's heart was pounding.

What did she mean?

He took a breath, tried to process everything clearly. In medical terms, didn't positive results mean a negative outlook?

Now he was sure that the end was near.

"Hi, this is Mr. Reginald Barrister. I'd like to speak to Dr. Johnston about my test results."

"One moment, please. The doctor will be right with you."

After half a minute, the doctor was on the line…

"Hi, Mr. Barrister. This is Dr. Johnston."

"Hi, doctor. You have the test results?"

"Yes. Your blood test showed an increased amount of monoclonal protein in your blood, as well as your urine. The skeletal survey corroborated that you have one lytic lesion in your arm. There are no other lytic lesions anywhere in your body. It is good that there is only one lesion. This indicates that your lesion is an isolated incident."

"Doctor. What is wrong with me?"

"Mr. Barrister, I cannot make a complete diagnosis until the bone marrow exam is finished. As discussed, I am sending your file to Dr. Kleuth, who is one of the finest hematologists in the area."

Reginald resumed his normal activity of delivering the mail. He was preoccupied with thoughts of his potentially failing health.

In the days that followed, he spent more and more time on the Internet. With every passing minute, he was more and more convinced that he was terminally ill.

Days later, Reginald received a call from the nurse at Dr. Kleuth's office She told him that the results of all the tests were back, including the bone marrow biopsy. The doctor wanted him to come in so that they could discuss the results.

Reginald felt paralyzed by the very thought of having to face the doctor.

Would he have to hear that he only had six months (or less) to live?

Reginald made an appointment for the next afternoon. In some ways, he actually felt relieved, as the tests were complete, and the results were now all in.

In twenty-four hours, he would know where he stood. Then he would be able to move on with his life, whether it was for a short period of time or for a normal, healthy lifespan.

The Barristers went to the doctor together. While they rode the bus, Loretta was her usual positive self. The optimism was exuding from her. She was almost like a young athlete who was confident that she would capture the gold medal at the Olympics. But her sunny attitude started to disturb Reggie's nerves.

"Loretta, dear, please. Don't be so positive. With your emotions up that high, you're going to have a major drop if there's bad news."

"Reggie, the news will be fine. I am confident of that,"Loretta said firmly

That was her way. She saw no reason to look at the glass as half empty, for what would the point of that be?

Reggie was starting to get really pissed about her gushing enthusiasm. He thought to himself: *How the fuck does she know that I'm going to be fine?*

Either way, in twenty minutes, they would know where Reginald stood.

When they got to the university hospital, they sat in the waiting room. Loretta chatted with one of the patients about gardening, while Reginald sat there, stiff as a board, nearly unable to breathe.

Finally…

"Mr. Barrister," the nurse called. "Please follow me."

Reginald and Loretta followed the nurse to the examining room. The whole way there, Reginald felt as if he was a dead man walking. The only items missing were the chains and shackles around his ankles and wrists.

Dr. Kleuth came into the offic with a young intern that he introduced as Marsha. Since it was a university hospital, it was very common for the doctors to bring in interns during a patient's visit. It was part of the educational experience.

Dr. Kleuth was a very intense man in his mid-fifties. He had a scraggly grey beard and looked much older than his actual age.

Without beating around the bush, Dr. Kleuth said, "Mr. Barrister, you have myeloma. It is concentrated in one area of your skeletal system."

"Oh my Lord!" Loretta exclaimed, gasping. She was completely caught off guard by the words uttered from the doctor's lips.

The doctor went on. "This diagnosis is better than multiple myeloma. However, it is myeloma and it has to be treated aggressively, as it could develop into multiple myeloma."

Reginald sat there in a daze. No words came to him.

And so the doctor continued, "This disease, you should

know, is treatable, but not curable. It is the same principle as diabetes, where you have to take medicine for the rest of your life. Currently, there is no known cure for the disease. With single area myeloma, we first perform surgery in the area that has the myeloma and remove the damaged bone. Next, we give you a round of chemotherapy for eight to twelve weeks to destroy the cancer cells. After that, we assess the situation and evaluate what further treatment may be required."

"Dr. Kleuth. I'm dying, right? This is an ugly diagnosis?" Reggie managed to say.

"Well, Mr. Barrister. I have patients that have had this condition and have been in remission for fifteen years, and others that went into multiple myeloma within one year. Even if it does go into multiple myeloma, there are new treatments that can extend the lives of patients. There are patients who have been alive for many years after they had stem cell transplantation," the doctor responded. "So let's focus on working to treat the immediate problem at hand and stopping the disease from progressing any further."

Reginald now knew where he stood.

By the time they got home, Loretta was a complete wreck. She started to tremble and cry uncontrollably.

"Reggie, my darling, I had prayed, and I knew that you were going to be fine. What happened? Oh God, what happened?"

"Loretta, we have to be strong. I am still alive, and we are going to fight this evil disease with every ounce of fight that e have, all right?"

Reginald had been right all along. Loretta, in the end, had been too optimistic.

Reginald scheduled the surgery immediately. Dr. Kleuth was not a surgeon, but he would be in charge of Reginald's care. He was indeed one of the top hematologists at the university hospital.

The surgery was performed within a week, and the doctors were able to remove all of the cancer. From there,

Reginald immediately went on to his chemo treatments. He was not able to work, as the treatments made him nauseous and extremely tired.

The spring came and went, and Reginald was able to tolerate the chemo as best he could. During the treatment, he lost his hair, and he also lost forty pounds. He even developed pneumonia, which, mercifully, was treated aggressively and cured.

It was now ten weeks after the initial diagnostic visit with Dr. Kleuth. During the intervening two-and-a-half-month period, Reginald had a lot of time to reflect on his life. He was young, yet he believed that he had lived a full and happy life. He was lucky to have such a dedicated and loving woman for his wife. She was always there for him, and her positive outlook on things made the journey all the more satisfying. Her support throughout their marriage was what made him love and adore her.

The twins knew that their daddy was sick, and they were scared of the thought of losing him. Of course, Loretta assured them that their daddy was going to be fine, and that he would be back to his strong self in just a few months.

Loretta and Reggie were shell shocked at this point. They did not know what the doctor was going to say during their next visit to his office This time, Loretta made no prognostication about the outcome. Reggie appeared worried, and he could see that his wife was worn down from this trying experience.

Dr. Kleuth entered the office with a smile on his fac

"Good news, Mr. Barrister," he said. "Your blood work shows no sign of the myeloma. It appears that the treatment has worked. Now, you will have to take the blood and urine tests every three months for the rest of your life. But at this point, I am going to declare that you are officially in remission."

Reggie simply could not believe his ears. He thought he was dreaming. Tears started to stream down his face.

He threw his arms around his wife and they both held onto one another, crying.

"Thank you, doctor," they both said repeatedly as they left.

Instead of taking the bus, they both walked home. Rather, *flew home,* held up high by the elated energy that they were both exuding. When they returned, they both ran up the stairs and allowed the babysitter to lea e.

Then, Loretta belted out to the twins: "Daddy is fine. Daddy is healthy. Daddy is in remission. This monster of a disease has been destroyed by the beautiful doctors at the university hospital."

The girls started to jump up and down and hug their parents. The scene at the Barrister house was unbelievable. Reggie had never thought that things would move in this direction. And he was going to bask in the glow of this happy state for as long as he possibly could.

Loretta screamed out to Reggie, "Honey, I am going to throw you the biggest party that has ever been thrown in the Bronx, and I am going to invite everyone we know. This is huge, Reg! This is going to be the celebration of your remission and the end of this scary disease!"

"Loretta, you know it could return at any time.

"Sssshhh!" Loretta exclaimed, putting a finger up to her lips. "I know it could; but for now, let's just enjoy the present and celebrate the positive with everyone."

"You're right, Loretta."

"I want to buy you a new suit, so that you look like a million dollars at this party," Loretta beamed.

"Loretta, you know we don't have the money to buy a new suit."

"Well. Today is your lucky day. When we were running back from the hospital, I noticed the Goodwill shop had some gorgeous suits in the window. So I don't want to hear anything. You deserve this; you deserve everything. We're all going to go down there and get the man that I love, the man that I adore, the man that I am going to spend many, many more happy years with, a spectacular get-up. One that is suited for the rich and famous!"

Reginald laughed. "Let's do it."

Part IV: Chapter Ten

"Now let us remember the six million people that died hopelessly in the holocaust. Their voices no longer exist and our voices must replace theirs so we can keep their legacies alive. Let us pray that the people on this planet will remember the Jews and Christians alike that were brutally murdered by the Nazis. We and generations to follow must never forget the atrocities of this mass genocide."

Aaron concluded his service at the temple. It was a beautiful summer day in downtown Manhattan. Many members of the congregation were at the shore or vacationing at this time of year, yet there were still about three hundred congregants at the morning's service. Many of the long-time members loved to come to that particular synagogue. Some of them were even the temple's founders. Fifty years prior, the congregation had started with twenty families and held their services in a local Methodist church.

Rabbi Berman had been the rabbi at the synagogue for forty years. Aaron had started thirty years into Berman's term, as the assistant rabbi. He proved to be a masterful speaker. Word quickly spread that his sermons were to die for. The congregation had grown significantly since he became the full-time rabbi eight years earlier. His style and manner attracted a younger demographic, which the temple desperately needed. He was able to do an outstanding job of fundraising, even developing a building fund that was used to expand the synagogue to accommodate twelve hundred people.

This was one of the largest reformed synagogues in Manhattan

As usual, Aaron did a fantastic job that Saturday morning.

Many of the congregants sought him out after the services to compliment him on his well-crafted sermon about present-day illegal immigrants and their interesting parallels to the Ellis Island immigrants from the early part of the twentieth century.

Aaron's wife came up and hugged him, congratulating him on a job well done. She had missed only two services since Aaron took over the reins at the temple. She was his biggest fan. Each time she heard him speak, it was like he opened a new door of excitement for her.

Aaron always appeared to be a high-energy individual. You had to be when you were the leader of a congregation that numbered close to two thousand people.

That Saturday was no different from any other. Aaron officiate over the congregation while he was high. He had been high at all the services.

Being a cocaine addict, that's just what he did. And he was able to adroitly hide it from his wife, family, friends, and the members of the temple. He regularly did a good job of camouflaging his whereabouts. The cocaine gave him the ability to perform at a level that no other rabbi could. This was his secret weapon. And his ability to get it every day was being funded exclusively by Louis, who had lent Aaron a great deal of money over the years.

Although the cocaine was giving him some pep, Aaron's habit was also wreaking havoc on his body. He was feeling burned out. He never let anyone know how he truly felt. He always gave the impression of being a strong, assertive, and empathetic leader who was available to the congregation 24/7. (Except, of course, when he was snorting the garbage that he was addicted to.)

After the service, Aaron went to lunch with his wife. In the middle of their meal, he told her that he had to prepare for a memorial service to be held later in the week. Marion nodded. She never questioned him. She knew that he had a full plate all the time, and that he enjoyed doing good for the world. What she did not know was that he was a drug addict whose habit was costing him more than $250,000 a year. He made a decent salary as a rabbi, but even that was not enough to support his habit. It was a good thing that he had Louis, who, all told, had lent him more than a million dollars over the past fi e years. Although Louis suspected that things were getting bad with Aaron, he tried to stay out of his business.

But one day, Louis received a phone call from Aaron's wife.

"Hi, Louis. It's Marion."

"Marion. How are you? Is everything okay?"

"Not really, Louis."

"What's wrong?"

"I'm concerned about Aaron. He hasn't been himself lately. He's very impatient and agitated most of the time. He looks like he is a walking zombie. His unusual behavior has not spilled over into his performance as a rabbi, but I believe it will, shortly. I know that something is terribly wrong."

"Do you want to meet for lunch?"

"Sure. When?"

"How about today? I can meet you at Rimino's on 13th Street at 12:30."

"Great. Thank you so much, Louis. You're a good friend."

Louis left the offic at 12:10. He took a cab to the restaurant, as he wanted to travel privately and did not want his driver to be involved.

Louis arrived about fi e minutes early. When he entered the restaurant, he could see that Marion was sitting in a corner table, away from the windows.

He noticed how striking she looked. She was in her late thirties. She had beautiful, long blonde hair, and her skin was fla less, with a pale tone to it. She had slightly rosy cheeks, which was her natural complexion; no makeup was needed for this beauty. But her biggest asset was her legs. Marion had the most amazing legs, and she did nothing to hide that fact. She was wearing a short mini-skirt that was about six inches above the knee. She was sitting with her legs crossed and sipping a drink.

The total image of purity.

Louis thought that Aaron was an immensely fortunate man to be married to such a magnificent creature

"Hi, Marion."

"Hi, Louis. Thanks for meeting on such short notice."

Louis smiled. "You know that I love both you and Aaron and would do anything to help you two."

Louis sat down, and on closer examination, noticed that Marion looked worn out. She had dark rings under her eyes. It also appeared that her eyes were bloodshot, either from too little sleep or too much crying

"Louis, I believe that Aaron is on drugs or that he has a major drinking problem. His demeanor has been erratic, and he appears to be tense all the time. We seem to be drifting apart. Lately, he keeps to himself and spends little time with the children. His routine now is to walk into the house, say hello, and then immediately go to his offic to get on the computer. He always wants to be alone. Everything is so private with him now. He has become a stranger in his own home."

"Why do you suspect drugs?"

She sighed. "When Aaron and I first met, he would smoke marijuana. And he mentioned that while he was in college, he tripped on acid and it made him feel superior. Well, his wild mood swings and his weight loss lean toward that conclusion."

"Perhaps Aaron has an emotional problem that needs to be treated..."

"Perhaps. But I suspect it's something other than that."

Now Louis took a breath. "Marion, what would you like me to do?"

"Please call Aaron. Ask him to seek help, ask him to get his life back on track. I want my husband back."

Louis and Marion both ordered chicken Caesar salads and Pellegrino to drink. They were out of the restaurant within an hour. After the initial talk about Aaron, the conversation was light, and mostly about family and the summer at the Hamptons. When they finished their food, Marion and Louis embraced and went their separate ways.

Louis decided to wait until the next day to call Aaron. He wanted to have time to formulate his approach. He wanted to rehearse his words before they were spoken.

When Louis arrived home that night, he discussed the situation with Donna, cutting right to the chase

"Marion suspects that Aaron is a cocaine addict. I mean, I knew he was doing cocaine on occasion, but I wasn't sure he was doing it all the time. His addiction is destroying his family life, and is destined to rip apart his professional career, too."

Donna's eyebrows shot upward. "Aaron, our friend and rabbi, is a druggie? How can that be? He's the *spiritual leader at our synagogue*."

"Shit happens, Donna."

"Maybe you shouldn't get involved. You should probably let the professionals intervene. This is too great an undertaking. Even for you."

He shrugged. "Aaron is my best friend, and I need to help him."

"Louis, I understand where you are coming from. I'm just having a hard time adapting to the contradiction of the circumstances."

"Look, Donna, we all have flaws. Aaron is a good and decent person. He has a sickness and needs to be helped. Drugs are an addiction. We need to give him all the guidance and support that we can."

"Louis, you are probably right. So…how are you going to proceed?"

"I'm going to call Aaron tomorrow and talk candidly

about this. I'm going to suggest that he seek professional help. We will see how the tenor of the discussion goes before I can say what I plan next. Maybe we'll have to do an intervention. We'll see."

The next morning, Louis arrived at his offic and did some routine deals. He was not looking forward to the phone call. It was Thursday morning, and Louis knew he could reach Aaron on his cell phone. At 10am, Louis finally phoned his friend

"Hey, Aaron. It's Louis!"

"Hello, Louis. My favorite friend, the Wall Street Mongol, the Hamptons resident, and the man that loves being on the fast track. Tell me, why do I have the honor of receiving your call on this fine day?

Wasting no time, Louis said, "Aaron, I think Marion knows about your addiction. She is very unnerved about it."

Aaron laughed. "What addiction might you be talking about?"

"Aaron, I know you're in denial, but you're on a path toward self-destruction. Come on, we've all seen you at the poker games."

"What is this, a fucking intervention? This is my life and you have no right to interfere. When I want your help, I will ask for it. In the meantime, just stay the fuck out of my affairs.

"I'm your friend, and you need professional help."

"Fuck you, Louis. Look: You lent me a large sum of money. You are as guilty as I am in this. You've been feeding this monster for the past fi e years. The blame has to be shared by both of us."

"That's not true. I loaned the money to you and Marion to help you out."

"Where the fuck did you think the money was going? Get your head out of the clouds, Louis. Did I buy a house? Do I live a lavish lifestyle? You never asked me once what I was doing with the money. Why is that?"

"Aaron, you're a friend, and I gave you what you wanted."

"Okay, Louis. So that means you're just as culpable as I am when it comes to my problem."

"So you admit that there *is* a problem?"

"Fuck you, Louis. You're not a friend. You're just a scumbag."

And with that, Aaron slammed the phone down.

Louis was stunned. He looked down at his hands and realized that he was trembling. The conversation had been a real tension convention. He had to leave the offic early and head toward the beach, so that he could unravel the stress that was now built up in his entire body.

Aaron was very upset over the call, although he *did* know that he was possessed by the drugs. In fact, the drugs had been doing all the talking during his phone call with Louis. Aaron was in extreme pain, and lately he inflicted that pain upon many people whom he came into contact with.

He could feel that the cocaine had taken over his being. He thought that Louis was a true friend, but at the same time he felt as if he were being treated like a child.

Aaron drove to a quiet park near the river. He sat quietly in his car and went about formulating a plan to end his life. He did not have any weapons, but he did have the white powder. He could take a larger dose, and never have to take that kind of bullshit from Louis ever again.

Aaron was not thinking clearly. After all, he was a low-life drug addict. Probably one of the only rabbis on the earth who was a cocaine addict. What a legacy to leave to his four children.

He sat quietly in his car. He thought about his wife, his kids, and how he had fucked up his life. There was no turning back for him. He had spiraled all the way down. He was depressed and not himself. Everything inside his head seemed twisted and clouded over.

Aaron went into his glove box and took out a large

portion of the white powder—three times the normal amount...

The pain decreased and was suddenly replaced by a rush of euphoria.

I am the scumbag; I am the low-life junkie. Yet when I put this lousy, rotten shit up my nose, I feel superior. I feel that I can conquer the world.

Things became cloudy, and Aaron disappeared off into a psychedelic experience.

A week had passed since Louis' phone call to Aaron. The rabbi kept thinking about calling Louis to apologize. His fingers would touch the phone pad, but he couldn't go through with it. He was too embarrassed to talk.

What would he do?

Without Louis, there would be no more funds coming his way. So what now?

Aaron conducted his usual affairs at the temple. He had to officiat at a funeral in the early afternoon and then pay a Shiva call to the family. On his way back from the congregants' home, he stopped at an ATM machine to see how much he had in his private bank account.

He saw that there was only $59,000 left.

This would cover only three more months of supply.

He had better get on Louis' good side before the well ran dry.

Desperation started to set in.

Louis was the rainmaker and the source of fresh cash.

Aaron walked slowly up the stairs to his apartment. They lived in a nice walk-up downtown. When he and Marion were first married, Marion's parents gave them the down payment to buy the place. They purchased it about eleven years earlier for about $450,000. Today, the three-bedroom, eighteen-thousand-and-fifty-square-foot place was worth about $2.3 million. A good investment indeed. If Louis didn't come through, then there was always home equity to recharge the battery

Aaron opened the door of his apartment and was surprised to find a group of people there waiting for him. He saw members of his family, along with Louis and Donna.

Aaron took a step back. "What the hell is this? What are all of you doing here? Has someone died?"

Marion moved toward her husband. "No, Aaron. Everyone is here because they love you. They all want you to get better."

"This is a bunch of crap. Whose idea was this? It was you, Louis, wasn't it?"

Louis just looked back at Aaron, not saying a word.

Aaron sighed an aggravated sigh. "I am not staying here. I am getting the hell out of this place now. I don't need your help. You think you're all perfect examples of humanity? What do you do that's so special? *I am a rabbi*!"

And then, Aaron stopped speaking. He realized just how distorted his angry sermon was. Sickness overcame his stomach, and he started to sob.

"Please, Aaron. Just sit and listen to what we have to say. If you don't like it, then you can leave. But at least listen to us," Marion pleaded. "Aaron, please stay until this is resolved."

Aaron looked around the room. He saw the people sitting around in a half-circle. Sitting in silence were his brother Jay, his parents, his sister Miriam, his oldest daughter Rebecca, his cousin Charlie, and of course, Marion, Louis, and Donna. There was also a woman in the room whom he had never seen before.

The female stranger looked warmly into his eyes. "Aaron, please sit."

Tears streamed down Aaron's face. "I am so embarrassed. I am so ashamed of what I have done. My actions have disappointed and affected so many people. I am the lowest type of living organism on this planet."

Aaron sat in a chair, surrounded by his loving friends and family.

The female stranger stood up and faced Aaron. "Hi. My name is Rabbi Sarah Feldman, and I am an alcoholic. I have not had a drink in ten years. I am currently a rabbi at a large temple in New Canaan, Connecticut."

Aaron took his head out of his hands and looked up in disbelief. *He was not alone.* There was another degenerate rabbi in the world aside from him.

Aaron's parents came over to him. They put their arms around him, and the three embraced like they used to do all the time when Aaron was a child.

Marion stood up, took a deep breath, and uttered, "Aaron, my love. Nothing matters more to me than for you to get better. You need to get your life back on track, darling. I grant you amnesty. You have to move on. You're better than this. You just got caught up. These drugs have taken away the very essence of who you are. They've taken your light away from you. But no more. It's time to shut it off. *Now.*"

After that comment, Aaron's brother and sister came to him and hugged him. They told him how much they loved and supported him.

Aaron stood up and addressed everyone: "I'm a failure. I have lied to and deceived you all. Why are you all trying to help? Wouldn't it be better for everyone if I just vanished?"

But the real tour de force happened when Aaron's nine-year-old daughter Rebecca got up and stood in the center of the room. She held a pad with notes scribbled on it. She looked directly into her father's eyes.

Rebecca was a small replica of her mother. She had long blonde hair, fla less skin, and a beautiful smile that could light up any room. With her flowing dress and matching shoes, she looked as if she was going to a bat mitz ah.

Rebecca took a deep breath. "Daddy, I love you, and I want you to get better. You have been a great daddy to me. You helped me with my homework, and you went to most of my soccer games. You even went to almost all of my school plays. Even the one where I played the part of a rabbit. And Daddy, I want to dance the first dance with you at my wedding. I want you to be there at my son's bris.

I want you to be part of my dreams. You are sick, Daddy. Please go for treatment, so you can get better.

Rebecca ran to hug her father. His arms wrapped around her. Aaron bawled uncontrollably.

"I love you, Daddy," Rebecca said through tears.

You could hear a pin drop in the room. Left and right, the tears were gushing out—so much so that there were water droplets on the hardwood floors

"Aaron, we are all here because we care deeply about you," Louis said.

"We love you dearly…Will you go to seek help?"

Aaron let out a long sigh, and his body seemed to melt into the floor. It was as if a huge burden had been lifted off his shoulders.

"I will get help," Aaron responded, his voice barely audible. He turned to look at Rabbi Feldman. "Tell me what I have to do, and I'll do it."

PART V: CHAPTER ELEVEN

Rose Geltman was very excited about her upcoming wedding anniversary. The glorious date was July 22. On that day, it would be Rose and Charles' fiftieth wedding anniversary. To celebrate, the Geltmans were planning to go on a two-week cruise to the Mediterranean.

It would be their first real vacation in years. Rose and Charles had worked very hard all their lives and had decided to retire about two years before. So they sold their small kosher neighborhood luncheonette to a young couple that had hopes and dreams of making a fortune at their new venture. The same hopes and dreams that Rose and Charles had had when they first opened the luncheonette forty-fi e years earlier.

But the business only provided them with the things they needed to lead a decent life. They were able to put their three children through college. The children were always well-dressed and, for the most part, received anything they wanted from their parents.

Charles had been the cook at the luncheonette, while Rose kept the books and handled all the other administrative duties, such as ordering the food and supervising the wait staff

The restaurant was a modest place that seated about sixty people. It was frequented by most of the local neighbors, as well as other folks that came to the area for their jobs. A lot of the customers were repeat customers, and Rose and Charles grew to know many of them over the years. The pair was regularly invited to the family functions thrown by many of their regular customers. The place opened at 6 am and closed at 3 pm, six days per week. With that schedule, it was hard for them to take time off for acation.

While they were working, Sunday had always been family day at the Geltman household. A day that Charles and Rose always cherished. A day away from the business. A day to pay attention to what mattered mos

Their restaurant business had dominated their lives for years.

They had worked exhausting hours. They had spent so much time listening to and taking action on customer complaints. The food was too hot, too cold, too overcooked, too spicy, too salty; you name it, they heard it. Charles, at one time, considered writing a book called, *Luncheonette Complaints*.

Charles was a big man; he was six-foot-one and weighed more than 200 pounds. He had developed a number of health conditions over the years. The fact that he had spent most of his life around food all the time did not help matters. Charles had been the number one food tester, as evidenced by his midsection.

Rose, on the other hand, was very petite and kept her trim figure, even at the age of sixty-seven. She only ate when she was hungry and was not compelled to eat just because the food was so readily available.

Their vacation was approaching rapidly. Rose was excited as she and her daughters headed to the mall to buy a few outfits for the cruise. That Saturday was officiall declared "Girls Day." Rose and her three daughters were going to shop from early in the morning until late at night.

Charles had never liked shopping. He enjoyed staying home and having the apartment all to himself while the women were out at the mall.

Rose had mentioned to her daughters that she had seen some nice things in the window of the local Goodwill shop. She wanted to stop there on the way to the mall to pick up a few things. But her daughters pleaded with her to skip the Goodwill and head straight for the mall.

Rose chuckled. "I know you girls are embarrassed and don't want to be caught dead anywhere near the Goodwill, but I don't care. I'm going."

The daughters continued to groan. They were not shy about expressing their discontent.

Rose smiled at her daughters. "Listen, girls: Your father and I have always been thrifty, so that we could provide for all of you."

Her youngest daughter sighed. "We know, Mom, but now it's your time to splurge!"

"Next stop…Goodwill!" Rose shouted.

The three daughters waited in the car as their mother entered the shop.

Rose noticed a few nice dresses that she thought would be perfect for the cruise. She also saw a suit for Charles, at a very reasonable price.

The old lady working there rang everything up for Rose. She ended up walking out of the store with three dresses and one suit…all for less than $150! Pleased by her purchases, Rose was grinning from ear to ear as she made her way back to the car. When she opened the car door, she could see the looks of embarrassment on her daughters' faces.

Rose was delighted with her finds but knew that her daughters would not be fulfilled until they did some significant shopping at the mall

"Next stop…the mall!" Rose shouted out.

With that, the car sped off to ard Yonkers.

Charles enjoyed his quiet time alone. He was watching the Yankees game, drinking a beer, and munching on some crispy potato chips. For him, this time alone was like Heaven.

When Charles was by himself, on occasion, his thoughts started wandering. He tried to stay focused and block out any negative thoughts. This obsessive pattern, however, would not be expunged from his mind. He tried very hard on this day to shut his mind's process down. But it was a losing battle, as the tsunami of thoughts was forcing itself upon his space and he could not block it from happening. The thoughts kept coming at him like a string of pearls; each frame of thought was a pearl, and with the string loose, the pearls just kept rolling off.

On this day, Charles was thinking about a horrific time in the past. He was thinking back to fi e years ago, when Rose had nearly died.

Charles did not want to go there, but it was too late. His thoughts had already enveloped his entire brain, suffocating him.

No, not that again. Please don't make me think of that day. Please, never again.

Charles got up, started to pace the room, back and forth. He could hear the noise of the game but could not quite follow what was going on. He was a man taken over by deplorable thoughts. The images would not leave, no matter how hard he tried. He struggled to redirect his focus. He thought about the upcoming cruise, he thought about the wonderful life he and Rose had together, and he thought about the graduations of each of his daughters—but these were only fleeting thoughts and would not stick to his cerebral cortex.

For that one horrifying day was crystal clear. It was almost as if it was happening in real time.

Evil was overshadowing good.

Charles could still see the faces of the intruders.

Two young men entered the luncheonette about five minutes before closing time. Rose was at the register, closing out the cash receipts for the day. She had neglected to put up the "Closed" sign and lock the door.

"We're closed," Rose told the men, barely looking up at them.

"Fuck you, bitch," the smaller of the men growled.

"Hand over that wad of cash and any other money or jewelry that you have!" the other man snarled, moving toward her.

Rose was in a state of disbelief. She stood there, frozen, just looking at the men.

The larger man took out a handgun and pointed it at Rose. "Do what we say, you old bitch, and you won't get hurt. Not too badly, anyway."

At that point, Charles emerged from the kitchen. "Is everything okay, sweetheart?"

With that, Charles looked up and saw for himself. His eyes filled up with fear and shock. He held his hands up. "Listen, guys. Just take what you need and go on your way."

The smaller man frowned. "Fuck you, man! We're in control here!"

The men grabbed Charles and tied him to a chair in the corner of the room.

"Stay there, you old bastard," the larger man said. "Watch and maybe you will learn something."

The men went around the store, making sure that all the blinds were tightly shut.

Then the smaller guy looked at Rose and flashed her a devilish grin. "Now we are ready for some seasoned pussy."

"Don't do it," Charles managed to call out, despite the fact that his throat was closing up. "I will give you anything. Take me, hurt me. Just leave my wife out of it."

"Shut the fuck up!" the larger man yelled.

The smaller one laughed. "Yeah, we know what we're doing. Your wife will love every minute of it."

The larger man gestured at Rose. "Now, bitch, stand in the middle of the room, so we can all take a good, long look at you."

Tears fell from Rose's eyes, and she started to tremble.

The smaller man was growing impatient. "Come on, bitch. Let's get naked."

Rose took all of her clothes off and stood in the middle of the room, totally humiliated. Wanting to intervene and save his poor wife, Charles started screaming and moving back and forth like a wild animal.

The larger man shook his head. "We gotta tape up his fucking mouth. I can't do this with him whining like a baby the whole time."

The men taped Charles' mouth and turned back toward Rose, who was still standing there, naked.

The larger man moved toward her. "Now get down on your knees and pleasure me, you slut. Make sure you finish the whole job, or I will blow your fucking brains out."

Rose stared into Charles' eyes for a brief moment, as if to say: Why us?

Charles looked back at her, extreme pain filling his face. He could not bear to see his wife in this position. But there was simply nothing he could do.

So the men had their way with Rose for a few hours, as Charles watched.

At the end of the despicable act, the larger man stood up and said to Rose, "I'm sorry, ma'am, but I'm always rough with my women. I just can't help myself."

With that, the larger man kicked Rose in the mouth, cracking three of her teeth. Blood started to pour out of her lips.

Charles tried to get loose and ended up bringing himself and his chair to the ground.

After the major blow, the larger man penetrated Rose for the last time.

The men left Rose on the floor bleeding, bruised both mentally and physically. They had been in the restaurant for a total of three hours.

Rose's wounds had healed after five years, and she'd moved on with her life.

Charles, on the other hand, never fully recovered from the events of that horrible day.

Those three hours continued to haunt him through the daylight hours. And in the night, when he closed his eyes to sleep, he still saw the faces of the two men, still saw the tears streaming down his wife's face.

For a long time after the horrific incident, although he did not share it with anyone, Charles had half a mind to blow his brains out. After all, who needed a brain when it was packed tight with so many awful thoughts?

And yet, at the end of the day, it was impossible for him to take his own life. He had too much to live for, even if he couldn't always enjoy these things at the maximum level.

So what Charles did was, he came to an agreement with the universe. Clearly, when that incident at the store occurred, the universe was telling Charles how mean and cruel and vicious it could be. The universe was looking at Charles and saying, "How do you like this, buddy? Pretty horrible, huh? Welcome to the Club of Lifelong Trauma Victims."

But Charles was not a stupid man. Far from it. Charles knew that if the universe had that much cruelty in it, then it had to have an equal amount of kindness. Someday, it would have to show him something wonderful—a miracle. Something unprecedented.

So, despite his obsessive thoughts, Charles worked up as much patience as he possibly could and waited for the day when the universe walked up to him and said, "Hey buddy, we've got a treat for you. We've got something that will help you to suffer a lot less...

CHAPTER TWELVE

Michael and Julia Thompson were high school sweethearts. It was love at first sight for these two, and the bond between them defied most people's imaginations. They were always together. They went shopping together, went to all the neighborhood parties together, attend d family gatherings together, and even went on trips to the local supermarket together.

It had long been a known-but-rarely-discussed fact that these two would someday be husband and wife. Michael worked part-time for his dad's construction company as a carpenter. He was a skilled craftsman and had little desire to go to college. He had found his niche in life and was very happy to be a tradesman. Although many of his friends would go on to college, Michael was content to be a carpenter for the rest of his life.

His dream was to someday have his own construction company.

Julia saw herself as being a great mom—probably a stay-at home-mom, all the better for nurturing her children and husband. She wanted to make certain that the family was central to her life's activities.

No one was surprised when the couple announced that they were getting married. The parents on both sides were delighted that their children had met one another and would henceforth spend the rest of their lives together.

They decided to live on Long Island, and they rented their first apartment in West Hempstead, a small town west of the Hamptons.

They stayed in their first apartment for a few years.

After the twins were born, they decided that the place was too small, and they had to find a larger place to li e in.

Michael was now working full-time for his dad's construction company. The firm built custom homes in the Hamptons, which was of course a very exclusive part of Long Island.

Julia, for her part, worked part-time as a secretary for a local mortgage and title company.

The two were living the American dream. Michael made a nice living, and Julia's salary was saved for the kids' college fund.

After some searching, they finally settled for a small cape cod in Holtsville, New York. This is where they would raise their family. The twin boys went to the local public schools, and Julia was very active in the community.

Michael's construction business was blossoming during the boom years. In general, Michael did not want to be in management. Instead, he loved to be hands-on, loved to work with his hands and see the fruition of his efforts almost immediately. Instant gratification was his thrill. He liked to get up very early in the morning, then work with strong sunshine beating down on him. He liked the way he looked, as well. Given the type of work he did, he managed to stay physically fit, whereas many of his friends had potbellies, smoked, and could hardly walk up a flight of stairs. He took pride in his appearance.

Sometime around the year 2000, Michael's dad, Martin, became very ill (his mom had passed on many years earlier) and the business started to wane, as his father had been the glue that held the operation together. While Michael turned away from management, Martin turned right toward it. The father conducted the bidding, went out on client appointments, and served as the liaison between the clients and architects.

When Martin died, the business ceased to exist in the manner which it had enjoyed during previous years.

The entrepreneurial spirit within Michael began to wane.

At his core, Michael still wanted to be hands-on. Indeed, he was able to secure some home building jobs on his own, though mostly because of his dad's reputation. He was content, however, for if he built one house a year on the Hamptons, it would be enough for him to make a nice living. He could, with Julia's additional income, live a comfortable lifestyle, pay for the twins' college education, and have money left over for their eventual retirement.

Life was good for Michael and Julia; they were living the American dream.

One night at dinner, Michael mentioned to Julia that he felt it was time to move up and buy a larger home. She was a little hesitant, as Michael was self-employed, and if he was injured or disabled, a larger home would put a financial burden on the entire family. Regardless, they agreed to at least start the process and start looking for a larger home.

Michael spent the next couple of months searching for a lot to build their dream home on. He found a third-of-an-acre lot that had been left over from a project that was complete. Because he knew the builder, and because their dads went back many years, the builder agreed that if Michael wanted the lot, he could have it for $450,000.

He crunched the numbers, and Michael felt that they could build a home on that lot for another $450,000, for a total cost of $900,000.

He and Julia sat down and developed their plan. They would attempt to sell their current house for about $450,000 and be able to put $300,000 cash toward the down payment on the new home.

It was virtually a done deal. They obtained the bank's approval on a $600,000 mortgage.

Their lifelong dream was shortly to become a reality. Of course, there were many more steps along the way. The major hurdle was to sell their existing house. This was 2005, however, and the Real Estate market was still very vibrant.

The house was listed the weekend after they got the

mortgage approval, and it sold within three weeks. Now the challenge was to find a place to live in during the construction phase.

Since the purchaser of their home was an investor, and he was going to use the home both as an income-producing property and for his own personal use, he agreed to rent the property back to Julia and Michael.

Now everything was set to go. The plan had been put into action.

The process seemed to go on forever, but after an arduous year-long run, the new home was finally ready.

Michael had built a beautiful 2,700-square-foot home just outside of the esteemed Hamptons. The twins were now juniors in high school and were starting to look for colleges. Where had all the time gone?

There were a lot of moving parts to their lives now: a new home, the kids shortly leaving for college, and then there was Julia's mom, who was not well physically. This required them to make many trips to the Bronx, New York, where she lived in the same apartment that she had been born in.

Many times, Julia had asked her mother to move in with them. Her mom refused, however, as she wanted her independence. Even though the Bronx was a challenging area, her mom still had her friends there and felt very comfortable and safe in her native neighborhood.

But after the move, given the new, large space, Julia felt that it might be easier for her to convince her mom to move in with them.

And so Julia begged her mom...numerous times.

Meanwhile, Michael's business had been thriving. He was very busy, and always had one house in his pipeline.

As a practical matter, if Julia's mom were to move in with them, their house would require some handicap upgrades to accommodate her needs. She had very bad rheumatoid arthritis, along with Parkinson's Disease.

No big deal. They both agreed that they would have

the house appraised and take out a home equity loan to pay for the additional accommodations for Julia's mom.

The appraiser came by, then within a week presented the family with an appraisal of $1,3000,000 on the home, which was $400,000 more than they paid for it just under a year and a half earlier! Michael was flat-out stunned when he received the email from the appraiser. To make a profit of that magnitude in such a short period of time made for a major coup. He left his office immediately

Michael ran home, burst into the kitchen, and announced to Julia, "How does it feel to be a millionaire?"

Julia blinked. "What do you mean?"

"Well, the bank appraised our house at $1,300,000, and will allow us to take out a home equity line of credit of $350,000."

Julia was nervous, but at the same time excited, as they only needed $100,000 for the handicap accommodations, but they could use some extra cash.

Some for college, some for an emergency reserve.

In the middle of 2006, a surprise occurred: The wheels started to come off of the Real Estate market. Seemingly overnight, things got very slow: Michael's business had one house to complete, and that was it.

He was nervous, but it was not panic time.

Everything they read pointed to a slight downturn in the housing market, followed by a quick reversal. The second part never happened, though. The Real Estate market collapsed, Michael had absolutely no work, and Julia was laid off from her job, as ell.

The tables had turned on them rather quickly. Both of their livelihoods depended on the Real Estate market. Skill-wise, Michael was purely a carpenter—such was all he knew. The twins were now in their first year of college, and the tuition was more than $75,000 for both of them. Their attendance in school was a point of pride, as both Michael and Julia were not college graduates, and the twins would be the first in their family to graduate from college.

They had no place to turn but to the home equity line of credit that they had been given a couple of years before, upon refinancing their home. This was their last resort. With mounting bills and no steady income, the only way to bridge the gap was to take on greater debt.

They were in their mid-forties and felt that the market would turn in a year or so, that they would be back on their feet in no time. In the meantime, Michael was not getting bids for any new homes, nor was he getting any calls for small carpentry jobs. Consumers were on hold, and this was the worst he had seen things in his entire career. Even though the government was saying that we were in a recession, for Michael and Julia it was definitely a depression—and a deep one at that.

In about one year, they completely ran out of cash, and only had a six-month reserve. They discontinued paying their life insurance premiums, and then next came their health insurance premiums.

They started to realize that they had to make a hard decision. Realized, moreover, that the recession could last much longer than expected. Things were very bad.

They sat down and discussed that they would have to sell their home and rent for the short-term, until they got back on their feet. They knew that the home had been appraised for $1,300,000 some years before and figured that it was worth about 1,100,000 million today. After commissions and closing costs, they could walk away with about $150,000, a nice tidy sum to bring some stability back into their lives, start off with some money in their pockets, and begin the rebuilding process.

Sadly, they had proceeded with the accommodations for Julia's mom, and yet the mom had still not committed one way or the other. So a great deal of their equity had been dropped into an uncertain proposition.

Michael called in a realtor to give them a market analysis. To their heavy shock, the realtor told them that their house was worth under $1,000,000.

They truly had no choice but to put it on the market.

In the next few months, they burned through their cash reserve and stopped making their mortgage payments. They both felt guilty about doing so, but what other choice did they have? The job that Julia had paid only for their food and utilities. At this dire point, the twins had to quit college, put their life's ambitions on hold, and go out to work to contribute to the family.

The house was on the market, and any offers they received were well below their mortgage. They learned a new term: they were "upside down" with their mortgage.

Michael got on anti-depressants. He had thoughts of suicide, but for now he was certain that they were only thoughts.

The realtor advised them to look into a short sale, and have the bank agree to take an amount less than the mortgage, then have them pay back this deficiency o er time.

Michael and Julia were reluctant to do this because it would destroy their credit. In the meantime, however, they were being served with papers from the bank that declared a forthcoming foreclosure on their home.

This was the United States of America! How could this be happening to them?

Where had the "land of opportunity" gone?

Soon, the local market became so bad that it looked like their house was worth about half of what they had paid for it. No question about it: Foreclosure was imminent. Michael spent his days talking to attorneys, accountants, and bankers to try to salvage what was left of their lives.

The bank finally agreed to the short sale, and all they needed now was an offer which was acceptable to the bank.

Julia decided to visit her mom in the Bronx for a few days. The time away from Michael was much needed, as the atmosphere at home was filled with tension, and rightfully so.

Julia took her mom for a walk. Her mom wanted to

visit the local Salvation Army store. Julia said, "Okay," even though she was not going to spend anything, as her family was officially destitut

As they were walking around the store, Julia noticed a beautiful suit in the back. She envisioned how great Michael would look in it. She fantasized about him wearing this magnificent suit to a construction job presentation, then getting a arded a million-dollar home to build.

She simply could not take her eyes off the suit.

She knew that she could not purchase it, but just for the heck of it she asked the store clerk, "What is the price of this suit?"

The clerk explained that it had been there for a while, and that she could have it for $35...

"It was given to us by some wealthy Wall Street type, and I can assure you, this is a very fine suit."

Julia's mom came by and asked, "Why are you looking at a suit? Is that for Michael?"

"Yes."

Her mother's brow wrinkled. "Michael does not need suits for his line of work."

Sighing, the cashier walked away.

"I know, Mom, but I was just thinking that maybe a suit like this would make Michael feel better and push him to be on top of his game when he goes for bid appointments, or if need be, job interviews."

"Honey, you really should not be buying this now. You are on a food and utilities budget, as sad as it may sound."

Julia broke down, hysterically crying. Right then and there, the whole burden of her life came pouring out of her. She was trembling, and she hugged her mom very tight.

"I'm sorry, Mom."

"There is nothing to be sorry about. You and Michael were dealt a terrible blow and setback, but you will recover. I promise."

The cashier returned: "Ma'am, is everything all right?"

Julia's mom reached into the bottom of her pocketbook, and with arthritic, trembling hands, she counted out thirty-fi e singles that she had won at bingo the night before.

She handed the money to the cashier and said, "Here, we will take this suit."

Julia looked at her mom with deep gratitude. A giant-sized box of tissues would not have been enough to stop the flow of tears at that moment

The woman placed the suit in a large box. Julia and her mom then headed back to her mom's place.

The next morning, Julia and her mom ate an early breakfast. Afterward, Julia headed back to Long Island. Something about the suit had uplifted her destroyed spirits; all the way home, she kept humming "Somewhere Over the Rainbow" to herself.

Upon pulling up the driveway, Julia burst into tears. She was starting to face the fact that everything really did suck for her and her husband.

Wiping her tears away, she cleared her throat and collected herself. She tried to draw more excitement from the suit. After she was sufficientl settled, she ran inside and said, "Michael, my love, I have a great surprise for you."

Michael was sitting and watching a football game near the fireplace

Which was now their main source of heat.

"What is it, honey?"

Julia opened the box and pulled out the suit. "Here we go, honey, this is for you for important meetings, and maybe some future job interviews. I thought you would look perfect with it on.

"Why don't you just take a moment and try it on?"

Mike went ballistic: "What kind of bullshit is this? I don't need a fucking suit! What I need is some work so I can be a man who supports his family!"

Michael wrestled the suit out of Julia's arms. They

both soon hit the floor. Julia was holding onto the suit, but Michael finally pulled it away from her. He rapidly stood up and said, "Here, this is what I think of your goddamn suit."

He then threw it into the fireplace.

"No! Michael, what are you doing?"

Julia got up from the floor and dashed to the fireplace. She pulled out the partially-burned suit. One sleeve and the inside of the jacket were charred.

Julia studied the suit through her teary eyes, breathing heavily.

She then blinked.

There was a burned envelope inside the suit's jacket pocket, partially hanging out. It looked like some type of letter.

No doubt it was probably destroyed.

Chapter Thirteen

The big day had finally arri ed!

Today was the day when Louis was going to make the cash distribution to the fi e people that had hopefully received his note.

He arrived at his offic early. There was a skip in his step. He was excited about tonight's dinner. Tonight, he was going to make the difference he had dreamed about.

His mind was swirling with questions.

What would these people be like?

What were their backgrounds?

Just how much would this monetary gift really affect them?

And most importantly, had everyone found the note?

He started to panic a little. What if someone who needed the money desperately had not found the note? What if they had never opened the pocket to find their treasure?

A few weeks earlier, Louis drove past the Goodwill shop and stopped in to ask the store clerk if the suits had been sold. She stated that the suits went very quickly to people that were from the neighborhood and had frequented the shop on a regular basis.

Louis was happy about that. At least if they were people from the neighborhood, there was a strong probability that they could really use that sum of money.

Louis concentrated on his deal-making and trades during the day. He put all of his energy into making the best deals, finance-wise, for his firm. However, he could not help but think about the night's event. He was nervous and excited. He had butterflie in his stomach and couldn't wait to get to the dinner.

Later in the afternoon, Louis called his wife.

"Hi, honey!"

"Hi, Louis. What's up?"

"What's up? Are you kidding me? What's up is that this is the day that I have been dreaming of. The day when I will make a major difference in the lives of many families."

"Oh, that. I almost forgot," Donna responded with sarcasm.

"So... I will see you at the restaurant at 7:30 pm sharp, right?"

Donna had planned to arrive at about 7 pm, just in case any of the guests came earlier. She and Louis had reserved a private room at Joe's Place. Donna was going to take a rented limo to the restaurant, while Louis would arrive directly from work and be dropped off by illiam.

Though Donna had initially been opposed to the idea, she had fully come around by now, had finally started seeing where her husband was coming from.

How much money did they really need anyhow?

They were already in the top 1% of the national economy when it came to net worth. So why not share their good fortune with those that were less fortunate?

It had started to rain a bit earlier. And for the balance of the day, the forecast was calling for showers and thunderstorms. But a little bad weather was not going to dampen Louis' mood.

Louis called his bank to make sure that the $5 million was ready for distribution. After discovering that it was, he leaned back in his chair, a huge grin spread across his face.

He had a feeling that tonight was going to be one of the best nights of his life.

Charles and Rose Nelson arrived back home, relaxed from their anniversary cruise. A couple of days later, they were getting ready for the big dinner

"Charles, are you going to wear the Armani suit to the dinner?" Rose asked.

Charles thought to himself for a moment. "I wasn't planning on it, but now that you bring it up…yeah, why not?"

"Great."

"You know, Rose, I am a little suspicious about this whole thing. Personally, I think it's a hoax. What bothers me the most is that the person writing the note asked for our bank account information. Maybe he's planning on robbing us or stealing our identity."

"Yes, but what if it's true, Charles? Maybe this person will put money into our bank account to help with our retirement. And maybe we can even help the girls out."

"Things like that don't happen in real life. They only happen in fairy tales."

Without missing a beat, Rose belted out, *"Fairy tales can come true. It could happen to you...if you're young at heart!"*

Charles looked at his wife as if she were from another planet.

Meanwhile, Autumn and her mom Susan were very excited about the dinner. They were like two schoolgirls getting ready for the prom. It had been months since Autumn's dad had passed away, and the wounds were slowly beginning to heal. Yet almost every time Autumn thought of her dad, she became engulfed in tears. She would then immediately direct her attention to the positive impact he'd had on her. She would think about the wonderful family outings that they'd had when she was growing up. Autumn was a very positive person. She was going to tonight's dinner to reap a fortune, and she had no doubts about the note-writer's intentions.

Just blocks away from Autumn and Susan, Ronald Lopez and his girlfriend Evelyn were now living together. Evelyn was the knockout Ronald had seen at the pharmacy. He had received some information about her and went on to pursue her relentlessly. After all, he believed her to be his soul mate.

Ronald was on his medication and was still working as an assistant computer operations manager at the oven manufacturer.

Both Ronald and Evelyn were talking about the evening, and how they were a little suspicious about everything. Of course, they were going to go with his Aunt Lauris, who was extremely positive about the upcoming event. As a matter of fact, she was already planning her trip around the world.

As for Reginald Barrister, he had been in remission for the past several months. Things were looking positive for him. He went back to the post offic to work on a "light duty basis" for the time being. His wife Loretta was just thankful that he was okay for now. They lived every day to the fullest, never neglecting to express their love for one another. Reggie planned to wear the suit that he'd bought at the Goodwill shop to the dinner.

Reggie and Loretta didn't know exactly what was going to transpire at the dinner, and they did not want to get their hopes up. They were just looking forward to having a fantastic dinner at Joe's Place. They had done research on the Internet and learned that it was one of the best restaurants in downtown Manhattan

Unlike Reggie, Michael could not wear his suit to the dinner, as it had been partially burned. Fortunately for him and Julia, the envelope inside had survived the fire. Upon plucking it from the fabric of the suit, the pair had found their breath slowing down and their sour mood lifting.

Now they just needed the goddamn invitation to be sincere.

The adrenaline was certainly flowing on that night. Although no one quite knew what to expect in that private room at Joe's Place, they were all eager to attend. The risk of not attending, of possibly missing out on the opportunity of a lifetime, was far too great.

Chapter Fourteen

As Louis wrapped up his day, he was getting more and more excited. He called William to remind him to be outside at 7 pm sharp. He also called Donna on her cell and found that she was already in transit from the Hamptons to the restaurant.

The plan was working smoothly. Like a well-oiled machine. Louis was going to obtain the bank account numbers from each person to wire the funds. At the dinner, he was going to distribute a promissory note to everyone, so that they would feel comfortable, knowing that the transactions were legitimate.

Louis went downstairs at 6:50 pm to wait for William in front of his building. William arrived at 6:55; early, as usual.

"Good evening, Mr. Bexton."

"Good evening, William."

"Let's get this show on the road. There's an accident downtown blocking our normal route. So we'll take the west side highway."

"Okay, let's roll!"

The car sped down the road.

William listened to the radio and drove, while Louis pounded furiously on his blackberry. The usual scene when they were together in the limo. Then…out of nowhere—

"Holy Shit!!"

"Oh my god!!"

The limo swerved to miss a garbage truck that had cut them off. They moved abruptly to the right, hitting and flying over the guardrail. The limo began to plummet into the East River.

William was wearing his seatbelt. Louis, however, had neglected to put on his seat belt, as he was too excited about the dinner.

The car hit the water with a loud splash and began floating in the ri er.

Not wasting any time, William undid his seatbelt and tried to move the window down. The electrical system had been destroyed, and the only way out was to smash the window wide open. William *kicked* the side window of the driver's side. He looked over, saw that Louis was unconscious—perhaps dead. He motioned to Louis, but there was no movement from his boss.

So William acted quickly. He was able to get the window open. Water was really starting to pour into the car now. They were sinking rapidly.

In his head, William thought to himself: *Oh my Lord. Please live, Mr. Bexton. Please live.*

William grabbed Louis and pushed him through the glass opening. Then he followed. He grabbed his employer tightly, and they both rose to the surface.

Once they were above water, William gasped for air and looked over at Louis, who was turning blue.

"Help! Someone, please help us!" William called out.

Some passersby who had seen the accident had already called 9-1-1, and the emergency vehicles were on their way. When they arrived, they worked quickly...

The coast guard had deployed a MedEvac helicopter, and from it, a life raft was lowered to William and Louis. The area that they were in did not allow for vehicles to park close enough to the water's shoreline, which was why a helicopter had been dispatched.

William and Louis were swiftly swept up from the cold water and flown to St. Luke's—a major Trauma One Center in the city.

William was in shock. He looked over at the paramedics

and saw that they were busy with Louis. There were four of them hovering over him, working at a frantic pace.

"Is he alive? Is there a pulse?" asked William softly.

Someone turned around and looked at William. "A slight pulse."

The helicopter landed at the hospital.

William was thoroughly checked out. They found that he had minor bruises and a slight concussion. They wanted to keep him overnight for observation.

Louis, on the other hand, was in bad shape. He had compound fractures and was placed on an IV. They had him hooked up to a breathing tube and had an EKG monitor attached to his chest. He as not conscious.

The doctors who were treating William wanted to know how to reach Louis' family. William gave the staff Donna's cell number.

Over at Joe's Place, Donna was waiting with all the guests.

Her parents were there with her. They were very close to their daughter and son-in-law, and really wanted to be a part of this special evening.

Everyone was sitting around the table in the private room. All making small talk. All nervous out of their minds. Donna asked each guest where they were from and how they had come across the envelope. She was amazed by each and every story.

Although everyone was making light conversation, they were all wondering what exactly was going to happen.

Donna kept watching the door, expecting her husband to walk in at any moment. But he was not showing up. This was very unlike him.

After nearly forty minutes of waiting, Donna spoke to everyone around the table: "I apologize to all of you. My husband is always on time; early most of the time, as a matter of fact. I'm going to give him a call to see where he is."

Donna called Louis' cell, and it went straight to

voicemail. She then tried William's cell phone, which went straight to voicemail, also.

She was beginning to get anxious. Before she could think of what to do next, her cell phone started to ring.

The number on the screen did not look familiar.

Donna answered it. "Hello?"

"Hello, Mrs. Bexton. This is Lieutenant Presley from the NYPD. There has been an accident. Your husband Louis was involved."

"Is he okay?" asked Donna, her entire body going numb.

"Ma'am, you need to go to St. Luke's on 23rd Street. You need to go there immediately."

"Oh, no."

Donna looked ashen as she hung up from the lieutenant.

Her dad noticed her sudden change in expression and asked, "Is everything okay?"

"It's Louis," she told her dad. "He has been in a terrible accident. We need to go to St. Luke's immediately."

Her father asked the restaurant manager to summon a cab.

Then he announced the bad news to the guests in the room. "Louis has been in an accident, so we're going to have to postpone the dinner."

Everyone stared at each other in disbelief. They did not know the Bextons, and they did not know whether this was a scam or whether this was really happening.

"What a bunch of bullshit!" blurted out Ronald. Then he caught himself and fell silent.

Charles had the presence of mind to organize a list of all the participants. He asked for everyone's contact information, just so everyone could stay in touch and keep abreast of the latest developments. After Donna and her parents left, Charles tried to assure everyone that every-thing was going to work out. He trusted Donna's sincerity, and he could sense that the Bextons meant well.

Although some of the guests did not quite agree with

Charles, they knew they had no choice but to wait.

Julia rubbed Michael's shoulder, seeing that his temper was beginning to flare.

One by one, they all left the restaurant, not knowing what fate had in store for them.

CHAPTER FIFTEEN

Donna arrived at the hospital with her parents. They were escorted right to the Trauma One section. There, they were greeted by Dr. Weinstein, a short, bald doctor with rosy cheeks.

"Good evening. I am Dr. Weinstein, the Head of the Trauma surgical unit. Your husband was in a bad automobile accident. His car plunged into the river. He has sustained multiple internal and external injuries. Right now, he is in surgery to repair a collapsed lung and a compound fracture of his arm. Does your husband have any medical conditions that we should be aware of?"

"Um…he has hypertension," Donna responded, her eyes watering with emotion.

"Do you know what medication he's on?"

"Zantac."

"Do you mean Ziac, Ma'am?"

"Yes…that's what I meant…Doctor, is my husband going to live?"

"Mrs. Bexton, we will do everything in our power to help him survive. He is at one of the finest Trauma One Centers in the world. Now, Louis had extensive injuries; he ruptured his spleen, punctured a lung, and cracked seven ribs. He's had multiple compound fractures and internal injuries."

The doctor explained to them that the trauma unit was trying to stabilize Louis, and that the next forty-eight hours were critical.

Donna's father got on the phone right away. He called Louis' parents and Aaron. Told them to get to the hospital as soon as possible.

Donna inquired about William. The doctor told her that he was okay and that he would be released from the hospital the next day.

Donna's parents also made arrangements for the babysitter to stay with the children, and they even informed Louis' office about what had happened

Donna was unable to visit Louis, as he was in and out of surgery. Since she wanted to stay close to him, she slept down the hall on a couch with her mom.

Every time a doctor approached, they would panic. Everyone was on edge.

"Mrs. Bexton, your husband is extremely critical, but stable," the doctor told Donna later that night.

"Will he live?" she asked him.

"It's too early to tell."

Donna could look into Louis' room, and also hear the sound of the ventilator. She yearned to hear the sound of his voice, to touch him, to smell his hair.

The next morning, Aaron arrived in the waiting room. Also present were Donna, William, Donna's parents, Louis' parents, and Louis' brother.

Today, visitors were allowed in the room. Everyone had to wear a gown and a protective mask, as infection was a major issue. Louis had enough complications, and the one thing he did not need now was an infection.

At one point, Donna's cell phone rang. She almost jumped out of her skin. Her hands were trembling, and she needed assistance to answer the phone. Her dad grasped the cell for her, held it up to her ear.

"Hello?" Donna said, her voice faint and full of exhaustion.

"Hello, this is Mario, the owner of Joe's Place. Is there anything we can do to help?"

"Well…you can pray for Louis, if you'd like."

"Which hospital is he in?"

"St. Luke's."

Later that day, Aaron assembled everyone in a circle outside of Louis' room. The rabbi looked rather thin and drawn. He had been out of rehab for a few weeks and was allegedly clean.

Aaron cleared his throat. "Let us pray for the recovery of Louis. Let us pray that he regain good health and that he live a long and fruitful life. Let us visualize the injuries that he has and let us visualize those injuries healing, so that Louis makes a full and quick recovery. Lord, please watch over this man and allow him to stay with us for many years to come. Amen."

"Amen," everyone repeated.

Aaron came over to comfort Donna, who looked as if she had been broken on the inside.

Everyone stood there silently.

Then, Reggie Barrister walked into the waiting room, moved toward Donna.

Aaron looked up at him questioningly. "Who are you?"

"I'm Reginald Barrister. One of the recipients."

"This is a family matter."

"I just wanted to meet a remarkable person. A man who wanted to share his good fortune with people that were in need. I've never met such a person, and I wanted to meet him before it may be too late."

"Only family is allowed in the room."

"I have a note. Can someone read it to him? It's from all the recipients."

Donna stepped toward Reggie, sighing. "Listen, we don't know what we're doing at this point. Giving you guys the money is not a top priority for the family at the moment."

Reggie smiled warmly at Donna. "I know. This is just something that all of us have written. We're all praying for the recovery of Mr. Bexton."

"Thank you," said Donna, as she took the note from Reggie's hand.

She handed the note to William, as she was not in the

right frame of mind to hold onto it. She dared not inquire as to its contents.

Forty-eight hours had passed since Louis had been admitted to the hospital, and he was still in a coma. He was in a medically-induced slumber.

Uncertainty gripped all of them.

As the hours passed by, the rabbi went into the room and spoke to Louis quietly. From outside of the room, everyone looked through the glass and watched. They could not see any movement from Louis.

"Louis, my dear friend, you're a good person. A *goota noshoma*. This should not have happened to such a person. You wanted to make a difference in the world, and you have. Your mere presence on this planet has made a differ ence to everyone you touched."

Next, Donna came into the room. She could hardly compose herself. Aaron saw the pain in her eyes and gave her a small, comforting nod. Then he walked out of the room.

Fighting back tears, Donna grabbed one of her husband's hands and said, "Louis, my love, my strength, my everything. Please do not leave me now. You have made a difference in this world, but now you must survive to fulfill your wish of helping those less fortunate than you. Please grasp your inner strength and rise above this horrible set of circumstances. Please, sweetheart."

Donna started to really break down, and her dad had to escort her out of the room.

Then William entered, clutching the note from Reginald in his hands. He looked down at his boss's motionless body, and tears started to well up in his eyes. "Mr. Bexton, you have been more than a boss to me. You are my mentor, and you are my idol. I love you. Now I want to read you something from all the recipients of your suits."

William opened up the note and started to read. "*Dear Mr. Bexton. We are very sorry to hear about the terrible accident. We know you have sustained some very bad injuries. But we also know that you will survive. We don't know you, but we do know a little about the fabric that holds you together as a human being. You are a special soul on this earth, and you wanted to make a difference in the lives of others. You have made a difference in our lives. We are all touched by your generosity. We want to be near a person such as you. A person that walks down the path of virtue…"*

William could not read any further. He lost complete control and broke down. Then he noticed something.

"Oh my God!" William cried out. "Mrs. Bexton!"

Donna hurried into the room, expecting the very worst.

"What is it, William?'

"Look!" William exclaimed, gesturing toward her husband.

Donna looked over at the bed.

Louis Bexton had opened up his eyes.

The author of this book has used a pseudonym.

Made in United States
North Haven, CT
04 November 2026

21770340R00092